W9-BEB-818

100

Ways to

Beat

the

Market

Gene Walden

Dearborn
Financial Publishing, Inc.®

TO THE KLEVE SOCIAL EMPIRE

Editorial Director: Cynthia A. Zigmund
Managing Editor: Jack Kiburz
Interior Design: Lucy Jenkins
Cover Design: S. Laird Jenkins Corporation
Typesetting: Elizabeth Pitts
Price board photo courtesy of Chicago Board of Trade

©1998 by Dearborn Financial Publishing, Inc.®

Published by Dearborn Financial Publishing, Inc.®

Library of Congress Cataloging-in-Publication Data

Walden, Gene
    100 ways to beat the market / Gene Walden.
      p. cm.
    Includes index.
    ISBN 0-7931-2854-4 (alk. paper)
    1. Stocks.   2. Investments.   3. Finance, Personal.   I. Title.
HG4661.W317   1998
332.6—dc21   98-19369
                                    CIP

Acknowledgments

This book would simply not have been possible without a lot of help from a lot of people. My executive editor, Cynthia Zigmund, helped shape the book with her ideas and suggestions. Managing editor Jack Kiburz, who has edited nearly every book I've ever written, proved again why he's the best in the business, doing another exceptional job of editing this book.

I also owe a great debt to several of the nation's most respected investment experts, who took the time to share their investment wisdom with me. In particular, I would like to thank Burton G. Malkiel, the Princeton professor and author of *A Random Walk Down Wall Street,* who offered a wealth of insights from his many years of tracking the market. I also would like to thank investment managers John W. Rogers, Jr. of Ariel Capital Management, James Barry, Jr. of the Barry Financial Group, George A. Mairs III of the Mairs and Power Growth

Fund, and financial publisher Mark Hulbert of the *Hulbert Financial Digest,* who took the time to offer their in-depth advice on the stock market. And I would like to thank a host of other outstanding investment managers who granted me interviews in the past that I drew on for this book, including Paul H. Wick, William Berger, Gary Pilgrim, Todger Anderson, Jonathan Schoolar, Fred Kobrick, David Ellison, Christopher Boyd, James Crabbe, George Vanderheiden, Roger Stamper, Lawrence Auriana, William Church, John Wallace, William Danoff, and Lee Kopp.

And finally, I'd like to thank David Koehler, a coauthor of mine on an earlier book, who helped shape many of my views on stock market investing that are reflected in the strategies and concepts covered in this book.

Contents

Introduction

Wall Street: A thoroughfare that begins in a
graveyard and ends in a river.

—Anonymous

It takes more than a good head for numbers to be successful in the
stock market. You need patience and persistence, and, at times, courage
and conviction. The dizzying twists and turns of the market have sunk
more than a few rookie investors who simply didn't have the mettle to
stick with their strategy. But those who continue to invest and diversify,
and continue to approach investing as a lifetime pursuit, invariably find
themselves richly rewarded for their diligence.

Investing in the stock market, after all, is not rocket science. High
school dropouts can succeed just as easily as PhDs. What trips most
people is that initial hurdle—the act of actually putting some money in
the market in the first place. Millions of would-be investors never succeed because they never try. They never take the money out of their
bank accounts and put it into the stock market, citing a litany of
excuses—"the market is down right now," or "the market is too high

now," or simply, "I don't know anything about the stock market." Nor will they ever know anything about stocks until they make that first investment. But years later, when the dust settles, almost everyone with the courage to take the plunge and invest in the market will look back on a lifetime of successful investing—not because they're lucky, and not necessarily because they're good. They will succeed, in large part, because over the long term, succeeding in the stock market is a heck of a lot easier than failing.

Here's why: Contrary to popular belief, investing in stocks bears little resemblance to gambling at a casino. At a casino, the odds always favor the house. But in the stock market, the odds favor the investor. Over time, the vast majority of stocks increase in value. In fact, the overall stock market tends to move up most years. In the period from 1983 through 1998, for instance, the stock market (as measured by the Dow Jones Industrial Average) set new highs 14 of the 16 years. That's not to say there won't be some ups and downs. There will be slow periods, volatile periods, and even dramatic declines in stock prices from time to time. (Experienced investors like to refer to those periods as "buying opportunities.") But those who invest for the long term clearly have the odds in their favor.

Since 1900, there have been four years when the market dropped more than 20 percent. But, there also have been 27 years when the market rose by 20 percent or more. Why do most stocks continue to increase in value? When you invest in a stock, you become a part owner in a corporation that is in business to make a profit. The corporation typically has hundreds or thousands of employees all working for you, striving each day to increase the company's sales and profits. And as profits climb, the value of the company increases, as well, which in turn boosts the value of your stock.

One key to beating the market is finding the companies that are growing the fastest. But there are certainly other factors, as well, that will contribute to your success, as you will learn in this book. The purpose of this book is to offer investors—both new and experienced—a simple, straightforward guide to successful stock market investing. You won't have to wade through volumes of technical jargon. There's no sophisticated strategies or complex number-crunching formulas to learn. The objective of this book is to present the art of investing in terms that are as succinct and easy to understand as possible. Most of it involves simple common sense.

This book is the result not only of my own research for the seven books and hundreds of columns, articles, and newsletters I've published, but also the hundreds of interviews I've conducted over the past 15 years with some of the world's top investment professionals. These include leading mutual fund managers, analysts, economists, authors, newsletter publishers, stockbrokers, money managers, and successful investors. The advice you'll read—sometimes contradictory—will help you shape your own personal investment strategy.

In many ways, the lessons of the market mirror the lessons of life. The stock market, after all, is a market of people—subject to the fallout of human fears and foibles. This book draws on some of the lessons of the market—and of life—to help you understand and profit from the psychology of the market.

Getting in the Game

1.

It is morally wrong to allow suckers to keep their money.

—"Canada" Bill Jones

Okay, let's get this over with. You paid the money; you bought the book. Now you want to know the answer to investing's eternal question: How can you beat the market?

Believe it or not, there's a method for beating the market that is so simple many investors would rather *not* use it because it takes the fun out of the game. It requires virtually no work, no thinking, and no decisions, and it can be summarized in a single sentence.

Which, of course, begs the question, What's the catch? After all, most Wall Street investment managers, roughly 80 percent, tend to trail the overall market average over the long term, despite devoting long hours every day researching companies, tracking the ups and downs of the Dow, and buying and selling stocks and bonds. So how can a small investor read one sentence and suddenly outperform most of the gurus on Wall Street?

Here's how you do it: *Buy an index mutual fund and set up a checking account deduction plan that automatically buys additional shares of the fund each month.*

Then sit back and watch your money grow. It's that simple.

Termed *dollar cost averaging,* the system relies on the volatility of the market to ensure that the investor automatically buys more shares when stocks are down and fewer shares when stocks are up. For example, let's say that you invest $100 a month automatically in shares of an index fund (index mutual funds invest in a broad selection of stocks that represent the overall market). When the market is high, and shares are trading at, let's say $25, your $100 investment would pay for four shares. When the market is low, and shares are trading at, let's say $14 a share, your $100 investment would buy about seven shares. So you're buying the most shares when stocks are low and the fewest when stocks are high (see chart).

And the real kicker is, you can do it automatically through a checking deduction plan, so the process continues to work without any physical, mental, or emotional involvement from you.

The question you may have is, if it's that simple and that reliable, why doesn't everyone do it? Why waste your time reading earnings reports, tracking price/earnings ratios, following the market, and agonizing over when to buy and when to sell, if you can use index fund dollar cost averaging with no effort?

Why? One word: BORRRRING!

Investors play the market because they enjoy it. Trying to beat the market can be fun, exhilarating, and exciting. You pit your wits against the gray suits of Wall Street, playing your hunches, making some buys and sells, wincing every time one of your picks takes a tumble, and gloating every time one doubles and splits.

It's a lot like gambling. Gamblers play the slots because they enjoy it. If time and energy were the issue, they would just pull up to the front door of the casino, empty their pockets, turn all their money into the cashier and drive away, instead of spending hours pouring coins into the machines. The final result would be the same, but with a whole lot less effort. But it's the involvement, the act of playing the game—and the rewards you get along the way—that keeps the people coming back for more.

Here's a challenge to those of you who enjoy playing the market: Set up two portfolios: a passive portfolio, using index-fund dollar cost averaging (you might want to invest in two or three different index funds to add still greater diversification); and an active portfolio using your own buying and selling strategies. Compare the results periodically and see which portfolio does the best. Unless you beat the odds, your passive, worry-free portfolio will earn more than your own actively managed portfolio.

The following chart demonstrates how dollar cost averaging can reduce your average share price. In the following example, the investor would have earned 6 percent over the market average by using dollar cost averaging.

Index Funds

To give you a head start in setting up a passive portfolio, here is a list of several of the more popular index funds, along with their fees and phone numbers. If you can afford it, you may wish to invest in two or three index funds to ensure even greater diversification in your port-folio. All the funds listed are "no load" (they charge no fees to buy and sell shares). They all offer automatic checking account deduction plans.

- Fidelity Spartan Market Index Fund: 800-544-8888
  The fund mirrors the Standard & Poor's 500 (S&P 500) Index.
  Annual expense ratio: 0.19 percent. No load if held 90 days.
- T. Rowe Price Equity Index Fund: 800-638-5660
  The fund mirrors the S&P 500 index. Annual expense ratio: 0.4 percent. No load.

Example of Dollar Cost Averaging
The Benefits of Investing on a Regular Periodic Basis

This example uses a typical one-year, month-to-month price swing of a stock to demonstrate the difference between buying a stock at its average yearly price and through dollar cost averaging.

	Jan.	Feb.	Mar.	Apr.	May	June
Share Price	$ 50	$ 55	$ 45	$ 40	$ 35	$ 42
Monthly Investment	$200	$200	$200	$200	$200	$200
Shares Purchased	4	3.6	4.4	5	5.7	5

	July	Aug.	Sept.	Oct.	Nov.	Dec.
Share Price	$ 50	$ 57	$ 65	$ 75	$ 70	$ 65
Monthly Investment	$200	$200	$200	$200	$200	$200
Shares Purchased	4	3.5	3.1	2.7	2.9	3.1

Total expenditure: $2,400
Total shares purchased: 47 shares (an average of 3.9 shares per month)
Average purchase price through dollar cost averaging (47 shares at $2,400): $51

Compare:
Average share price during the 12 months: $54
Savings through dollar cost averaging: $3 per share (6 percent)

- Invesco Index Fund: 800-525-8085

  The fund just opened in 1998. Expense ratios have not been established. No load.

- Scudder S&P 500 Index Fund: 800-225-2470

  The fund recently opened, charging an annual expense fee of 0.4 percent. That may be subject to change. No load.

2.

Ready, fire, aim.

—Harry Levinson

If you're new to investing, the first challenge you'll face in your battle of wits with the stock market has nothing to do with the whims of Wall Street. The first challenge is to overcome inertia: Take action. Get in the game. The best way to start investing is the Nike way: *Just do it*. Pick a stock, whatever strikes your fancy, open a brokerage account, and place your order. It is irrelevant whether the market is high or low, or whether the economy is up or down. The important thing is to just get started. Only then does the real learning begin.

Here's an action plan:

1. Open up an account with a brokerage firm. If you plan to make your own stock picks, use a discounter and save on commissions. A standard buy or sell commission through most discounters would cost about $30 to $50. Online discount

commissions are as low as $8 per transaction. By comparison, a full-service broker would charge about $70 to $100 per standard stock transaction.

2. Pick a stock.
3. Place your order.
4. Watch and learn, and repeat steps two and three.

Don't worry about your inexperience. Even America's most successful investment managers were inexperienced novices at one point in their lives. But they took the first step, bought their first stock, and began to learn how the game was played. Investing is no different than any other pursuit. You can follow sports for years, watch it on TV, and read about it in the newspaper, but until you lace up the Nikes and get in the game, you cannot possibly understand how it's played. Similarly, you can follow investing from the sidelines, read some books, attend some seminars, and watch the financial news, but the only way to learn the real lessons of the market—the emotion, the discipline, the execution—is by putting your own money on the line.

3.

Every young man should have a hobby.
Learning how to handle money is the
best one.

—Jack Hurley

It's not just the money that keeps some people out of the stock market. It's the emotions—the fear of the unknown and the apprehension over the drudgery of dealing with stock tables, earnings reports, account statements, and the whole messy scene of financial responsibility.

The problem is in the approach. Rather than to see investing as drudgery, approach it as a hobby or a game—Monopoly with real money. As your portfolio grows, so will your interest in the game. Soon you'll find yourself trading stocks, hunting for bargains, scouting for hot tips, joining investment clubs, comparing your performance with your friends, and crafting your own strategies to land that next big winner.

"The stock market had always been a hobby of mine growing up," says John W. Rogers, Jr., president of the highly ranked Ariel Mutual Funds. "I always loved stocks. I guess that's why I ended up in the investment business."

The more involved you become, the more money you'll make, and the more fun you'll have—particularly during bull markets. No longer will it be drudgery to read through the stock tables and see your picks bounding to new highs, to look through your earnings reports and see your companies growing quarter by quarter, and to open your account statement and see your net worth climbing steadily. That's when you become hooked on the stock market game. It becomes your pastime for life.

4.

If I had to live my life again, I would make the same mistakes, only sooner.

—Tallulah Bankhead

Fact: All your stocks will not go up.

You will make countless errors in judgment and timing that will cost you thousands of dollars. You will buy stocks that suddenly go down. You will sell stocks that suddenly go up. It's all part of the trial and error of the stock market game. To learn is to lose. But the sooner you start making your mistakes, the sooner you'll start making money. In the end, the law of averages will bail you out. Your own persistence, and the market's rocky but inevitable ascent, ultimately will conspire to put large sums of money in your investment coffers.

"The only certainty about the stock market is that there is none," says George Vanderheiden, fund manager of the highly rated Fidelity Advisor Growth Opportunities Portfolio. "Every successful investor constantly makes mistakes. Don't be afraid of failure. While Babe Ruth had 714 homers, he also had 1,330 strikeouts."

No one beats the market every year. No one hits a home run with every swing. But to succeed in the market you have to keep stepping up to the plate. Amid your failures will come great successes. The sooner you begin, the sooner you win.

5.

A blindfolded chimpanzee throwing darts at the *Wall Street Journal* could select a portfolio that would do as well as one carefully selected by the experts.

—Burton G. Malkiel, *A Random Walk Down Wall Street*

In his investment classic, *A Random Walk Down Wall Street,* Burton Malkiel devotes nearly 500 entertaining pages to debunking virtually every popular theory of stock selection employed by the gurus of Wall Street. Malkiel, a Princeton professor, first published *Random Walk*—and his dart-throwing chimp theory—in 1973 amid much controversy. But the book has survived to its sixth edition, and Malkiel still sticks to his premise, insisting that time has proven him out.

"I don't literally mean you should throw darts," explains Malkiel, "but a passive approach has, in fact, over time, outperformed between two-thirds and 75 percent of actively managed portfolios."

Investors may read a sense of hopelessness into Malkiel's message, but he is actually very bullish on the stock market. He just believes that investors could find a better use for their time than poring over annual reports, balance sheets, and other research materials to try to get an edge on the market. Instead, Malkiel recommends simply buying index funds, which invest in a broadly diversified portfolio designed to mirror the overall market. Malkiel points out that index funds typically outperform the majority of actively managed mutual funds. "While I grant you there are active portfolios that outperform," he explains, "they are not the same from year to year, and there's no way you can know in advance who they're going to be."

The biggest problem with strategies for beating the market averages, says Malkiel, is that as soon as they become known to investors, the market adjusts to render them useless. "Suppose, for example, there truly is a dependable January effect, that the stock market will rally in the first five days of January," says Malkiel. "What will I do? I'll buy late in December, on the last day of December, and sell on January 5. But then, we'll find that the market rallied the last day of December and because there was so much selling on January 5, we would have to sell on January 4 to take advantage of this effect. Thus, to beat the gun, I'll have to be buying earlier and earlier in December and selling earlier and earlier in January so that eventually the pattern will self-destruct."

It's Malkiel's contention that stocks are almost always priced fairly relative to the information currently available on those stocks. That's what is known as the "efficient market theory." It's this efficient market that evens the playing field for all investors. Malkiel contends that at any given time, stock prices "fully reflect all known information, and even uninformed investors buying a diversified portfolio at the tableau of prices given by the market will obtain a rate of return as good as that achieved by the experts."

One theory that Malkiel shoots down is the perception that riskier stocks bring higher returns. Malkiel defines risky stocks as those with high volatility. There is a measure of volatility in the stock market known as "beta." The higher the beta, the more volatile the stock. Some investors have assumed that the higher beta stocks, while more volatile in the short term, offered better average long-term returns. But Malkiel cites a 1992 study by Eugene Fama and Kenneth French that showed absolutely no correlation between beta and performance. Malkiel also conducted his own study of high beta stocks, and found that "the highest beta portfolios had the lowest returns. What is very clear," he continues, "is that if you thought you could get a dependably higher rate of return by buying a high-beta portfolio, you would have been badly disappointed."

He shoots down several other timeworn theories as well. He admits that there may be some seasonal patterns in the stock market, that stocks with low price-earnings ratios can sometimes outperform the market, and that there may be some evidence of short-run momentum in the market, but he contends that closer analysis reveals that there is no consistently reliable pattern for any of those theories. He also takes to task the theory that you can earn a higher rate of return by buying stocks with a relatively high dividend yield. "This phenomenon does not work with individual stocks. We tried simulating strategies. If you simply purchase a portfolio of individual stocks with the highest dividend yields in the market, you will not earn a particularly high rate of return."

That's why Malkiel believes that the easiest way to play the market is to buy a broad cross section of index funds that mirror the overall market. "Indexing allows investors to buy securities of all types with no effort, minimal expense, and where relevant, with considerable tax savings."

What is clear is that no single investment strategy will bring you above-average returns every single year. To play the market successfully, you will need a combination of investment strategies, the patience and conviction to see you through the down times, a modicum of luck, and the courage to buy when stocks are down and everyone else is fleeing to the sidelines.

6.

If a monkey can invest as well as a professional, or nearly so, it stands to reason that you can too.

—Andrew Tobias, *The Only Investment Guide You'll Ever Need*

Despite the odds, thousands of active investors do outperform the market over a lifetime of investing—sometimes by accident, and sometimes through an informed, disciplined investment program.

Investing is not rocket science. It's not nuclear physics. You don't have to be a genius to succeed in the market. All you need is an interest in making money and a willingness to stick it out for the long term. If you try, you will succeed. A monkey can do it. So can you.

7.

The weak have one weapon: the errors of those who think they are strong.

—Georges Bidault

So now you know. Those confident, collected, finely attired stock market specialists on "Wall Street Week" who seem to have all the answers to Louis Rukeyser's probing questions are really just faking it. The emperor has no clothes. The big guns responsible for moving billions of dollars in the stock market are just as susceptible to mistakes as your typical chimpanzee throwing darts at the stock tables.

And when the big guns make their mistakes, you, the little guy (or gal), can cash in by swooping up the bargains they leave in their wake. "We wait for the market to hand us the stock on a bad day," says Michael Price, Manager of the Franklin Resources Mutual Series Funds. "When we see a very large problem with a company and the stock drops by 25 to 50 percent, that's when we start getting involved."

Does that mean you should see every battered stock as an opportunity? Not exactly. When stocks fall, there's usually a reason. From an investor's point of view, some reasons are better than others.

"Ninety percent of the stocks go down for the right reason," says James Crabbe, manager and founder of the Crabbe Huson Special Fund. "We want to find the other 10 percent."

Let's say the market has been moving up at a brisk pace, and a stock you're interested in buying has raced to an all-time high. Do you buy it at that price, or do you wait? If you're patient, you'll probably be able to buy the stock a few dollars cheaper later. And not because of any flaw in the company or its earnings, but due simply to the normal ebb and flow of the stock market. The overall market, and the vast majority of individual stocks within it, move in broad, uneven swings. Even in bull markets, stock prices are constantly in flux. The market moves up, corrects, moves up, and corrects again. Exhilarating rallies can be quickly followed by breathtaking free falls. It's after those corrections—when the market and the stock you're following sink a few percentage points—that you can buy your pick a few points cheaper.

As a small investor, you can move nimbly through the market, taking advantage of the overreactions of the big institutional traders to buy your stocks at a discount.

8.

Traffic signals in New York are just
rough guidelines.

—David Letterman

The whole concept of using the Dow Jones Industrial Average
(DJIA, or the "Dow") as a "representative" sample of the overall market is really just a sham, a ruse, a fake. Because, like traffic signals in
New York, Wall Street's DJIA is really just a rough guideline. If you
use it as a point of reference to compare your returns with the overall
market, you're really cheating yourself. By no means is the Dow an
accurate barometer of the overall market.

To be fair to those who created the Dow, it was never intended to
perfectly mirror the market. It was only intended to be a rough guideline
of how industrial stocks were faring. No utility stocks and no transportation stocks are listed in the DJIA. In fact, the Dow consists of only 30
stocks in all. And, far from being a representative sample, many of the
stocks on the list are the cream of the crop of their specific industries.

For instance, most tobacco-related stocks have lagged the market for several years, but the industry's lone representative on the DJIA, Philip Morris, has had exceptional growth for many years, dramatically outperforming all other tobacco stocks. Other DJIA members such as Merck, McDonald's, General Electric, Coca-Cola, IBM, AT&T, Boeing, 3M, Walt Disney, and Procter & Gamble would all be considered leaders in their industries. These are *not* average stocks.

Besides featuring industry leaders and omitting certain slow-moving sectors, such as utilities, other factors skew the average as well. The Dow is "price-weighted." In other words, higher priced stocks affect the movement of the Dow more than lower priced stocks. In fact, the movement of the highest priced stocks on the list can have more than twice the effect on the overall average than the movement of the lowest priced stocks. The system is an arbitrary and irrational way to compute the market average.

On top of that, because of the index funds and other investment strategies that are tied to the Dow, the 30 stocks that make up the index are artificially inflated. Many investors buy and hold the stocks of the DJIA (or mutual funds that invest in those stocks) simply because they are included in the index.

This isn't just an idle theory. The numbers bear it out. From 1990 through 1997, the DJIA climbed 187 percent. By comparison, the Dow Jones Utility Index moved up just 4 percent, the Standard & Poor's 500, an index based on 500 blue chip stocks, rose 175 percent during the same period, and the New York Stock Exchange Composite Index rose just 152 percent.

So if you don't beat the Dow, don't sweat it. The cards really are all stacked against you.

9.

As always, victory finds a hundred fathers,
but defeat is an orphan.

—Count Galeazzo Ciano

If you're relatively new to the stock market, you may find yourself wondering what you're doing wrong—why you continue to have mixed results with your stocks while everyone around you seems to pick nothing but winners for their portfolios. Well, guess what? They're not. They only talk about the winners. Their losers simply don't make it into the conversation. It's a subject too painful to discuss.

Accentuating the positive is human nature. The golfer who shoots 30 over par isn't going walk into the clubhouse and start talking about his or her game. More likely, that golfer will have a quiet drink in the corner. But take 30 strokes off that score, and everyone in the clubhouse would hear about it. No one wants to talk about their failures— only their successes. So don't get discouraged when you hear your friends boast about their big winnings in the market. You're only hearing half the story.

10.

There are three kinds of people:
those who can count and those who can't.

—Bumper sticker

Once upon a time, 16 sweet-faced ladies stumbled upon a magical formula for picking stocks that was so simple and so effective it attracted hundreds of thousands of devoted converts.

Far from the confusing din of Wall Street and the ivory-covered halls of academia, these 16 rural Midwestern ladies wove together an investment system so revolutionary that it outperformed all the systems ever conceived by the world's brightest economists and academics. As the ladies proudly reported, their system produced a ten-year return from 1983 to 1993 of 23.4 percent per year—more than twice the rate of the Dow Jones Industrial Average and far ahead of all of Wall Street's sharpest money managers.

The ladies happily shared their secret formula with anyone who would buy their books, tapes, or video.

Soon the 16 sweet-faced ladies were the toast of the media. "Looking for proof that you needn't work on Wall Street to beat the market?" gushed *Newsweek*. "Meet the Beardstown ladies."

Readers of their books also were reverent in their praise. "It could easily become the bible for beginning stock investors," wrote one reader in an Internet review. "It certainly worked for me!"

"It inspired 45 women in my small town to form three clubs," wrote another reader.

The Beardstown ladies' revolutionary concept spawned a veritable cottage industry of investment products. Nearly a million copies of *The Beardstown Ladies Common Sense Investment Guide: How We Beat the Stock Market—And You Can Too* have been sold. There's an audiotape by the same name and a video called *Cookin' Up Profits on Wall Street,* as well as a collection of related books, including *The Beardstown Ladies' Little Book of Investment Wisdom.*

What was the secret of the Beardstown ladies? How did these stock market novices attain such incredible returns? The secret, as it turned out, had nothing to do with investment strategy. The secret was simply that the ladies couldn't count. They used a flawed method to calculate their returns and came up with a figure that grossly overstated their performance. In truth, their performance didn't even match the market—not even close.

They claimed a ten-year return of 23.4 percent per year, but their actual return was considerably less—an anemic 9.1 percent, according to a recent audit of their records by Price Waterhouse. Their return fell well below the Dow Jones Industrial Average, which grew about 11.5 percent per year. In other words, a monkey throwing darts at the stock tables would have outperformed the Beardstown ladies.

In investing, there are no simple answers—and no magic formulas. Next time a sweet little lady whispers in your ear that she can get you twice the market average, kindly decline the opportunity. Get your advice from someone who can count.

11.

You can't win gambling with your hands
in your pockets.

—Old adage

The worst excuse I've ever heard for refusing to invest in stocks
is the old line, "Well, the market's kind of down right now, isn't it? I'd
rather wait until things turn around."

That's like saying "I'd really like to buy a new suit, but Macy's has
that ridiculous 30 percent off sale going on right now, so I think I'll
wait. When prices get back to normal, then I'll go back in and buy the
suit." The stock market is one of the only venues of commerce in which
consumers actually shrink away from the bargains. When stocks are on
sale, that's the time to buy.

There is always uncertainty in the market, with every stock and
every sector. Recently on a financial cable talk show, I was asked about
one of the top stock picks in my book, *The 100 Best Stocks to Own in
America* (Dearborn Financial Publishing, 1998). It was a bank stock
that had done very well over the past ten years. But the interviewer

questioned the timeliness of the pick, suggesting that if interest rates should take a sudden upward turn, that could hurt the prospects for the company.

"Yes, yes," I answered. "That could happen. The wolf is always at the door. Every day, every week, every month, every year, interest rates could go up and bank stocks could go down. And with every stock and every sector, you could find a similar wolf at the door ready to spoil a stock's peaceful ascent."

But if you worry about every possible negative element that could affect a stock, you might never invest in stocks at all. At some point, if you're going to make it in the stock market, you have to get over your fears and put your money on the table. You wouldn't get very far in poker if you assumed on every hand that one of your opponents might have four aces. You'd never bet, no matter how strong your hand. The smart gambler knows you have to play the averages. You assume you will lose some hands, just as you assume that some of your stocks will drop from time to time. But most of the time, the blue chip stocks in your portfolio will provide very solid returns. The greater evil is to let your fears keep you out of the market.

If you want to make money in the market, you've got to ante up and play the game. Over time, your valor will be rewarded.

12.

Save a little money each month, and at the
end of the year you'll be surprised at how
little you have.

—Ernest Haskins

You can't make big money in stocks by throwing dimes and
nickels at the market. To reach your retirement years with a substantial
nest egg, you need to invest substantial sums along the way.

And the older you are when you begin, the more you will need to
invest each year. For instance, to reach $1 million by age 65 (assuming
an average annual return of 11 percent per year), a 19-year-old investor
could meet that goal by investing just $1,000 a year. But a 40-year-old
would have to invest nearly $10,000 a year to reach $1 million by
retirement.

How much do you need to invest each year to reach your goals?
The following chart should help you decide.

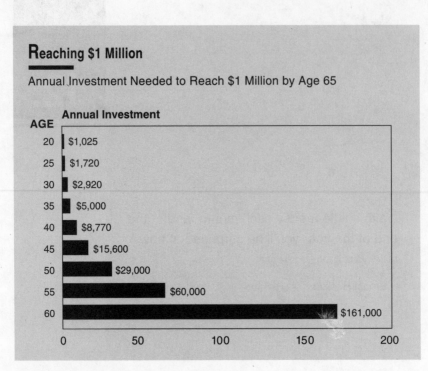

Reaching $1 Million

Annual Investment Needed to Reach $1 Million by Age 65

Based on average stock growth of 11% per year

13.

The secret of financial success is to spend
what you have left after saving, instead of
saving what you have left after spending.

—Anonymous

For those middle-aged working people who just read the last chapter—and are now shell-shocked to learn that you may need to sock away ten grand a year to reach $1 million by retirement—please do not despair. You may be overlooking some other factors.

For instance, when you retire, you will probably be able to draw some Social Security to help pay the bills, and you might also have a pension from your employer. Your expenses also are likely to decline after you retire. By then, you probably will have paid off your mortgage, so you won't be strapped with regular monthly house payments. Your kids probably will be out of school and (presumably) out of your house. You won't have the usual transportation costs associated with the daily commute to work, and you probably will have less of an appetite for the latest clothing and consumer products. So your living expenses should be considerably less in retirement than they are in your working years.

On top of that, there's obviously no rule that says you have to save $1 million by the time you retire. You might see $1 million as a goal, an objective to shoot for, but if you come up short, you'll still survive.

Just the same, the ideal situation would be to reach your retirement years with all the money you'll need to live comfortably. And to do that, you may have to set some priorities. It may mean that you need to make a career change. Drastic as that may seem, if you're slaving away for 40 or 50 hours a week year in and year out with no hope of reaching a prosperous retirement, changing careers may be the only option that makes sense.

A tighter budget and wiser spending priorities also may help. A recent survey of consumers revealed that while building a nest egg for retirement was the number one long-term financial goal of most Americans, retirement savings ranked 15th among short-term goals. In other words, we want the money there when we're ready to retire, but in the meantime, there are 14 other things we'd rather spend it on—better clothes, better car, better furniture, better stereo, better kitchen, bigger house, and so on.

Sure, you deserve some of the finer things in life, and you should work toward getting those things. But the vast majority of working Americans need to put retirement savings much higher on the priority list.

14.

A stockbroker is someone who invests your
money until it is all gone.

—Woody Allen

One way to get more return from your investment dollars is to cut out the middleman. There are about a thousand U.S. companies that sell their stock directly to shareholders with no commission. These are programs your broker will never tell you about.

Termed "dividend reinvestment and stock purchase plans" (DRIPs for short or "stock reinvestment plans"), these plans enable shareholders not only to reinvest their dividends in additional shares automatically, but also to buy more stock in the company, commission-free.

While some company plans set modest limits for the cash contribution, such as $1,000 a month, other companies have instituted very liberal contribution policies. American Home Products allows shareholders to invest more than $100,000 a year in the commission-free program. PepsiCo, Warner-Lambert, Coca-Cola, and Anheuser-Busch all allow contributions of up to $60,000 a year. May Department Stores puts no upper limit on its program.

If there is a downside to DRIPs, perhaps it's the fact that you have no control over when the stocks are purchased. Most companies have a date set each month or each quarter (depending on how the plan is set up) to make all shareholder stock purchases.

To enroll in most DRIP plans, you must already own shares of the company stock (which you have to buy through a brokerage company). But a small, growing number of companies are beginning to offer programs that allow even new investors to buy shares directly through the company.

DRIPs are perfect for investors who want to build a position in several companies at the same time with relatively small monthly contributions—and without getting killed by brokerage commissions. The minimum contribution limits range from about $10 to $50 per payment, depending on the company. And, if you wish, your monthly or quarterly contributions can be deducted automatically from your bank account. It's no way to treat your broker, but it's a great way to get the most from your investment dollars.

Covering the Bases

15.

If you want to make it in show business,
get the hell out of Oregon.

—Sophie Tucker (to Johnnie Ray)

If you want to get rich and stay rich, there's only one clear way to do it. "Be an owner, not a lender," says James A. Barry, an investment manager and host of the PBS show, "Financial Success." "You cannot buy CDs, Treasury bills, Treasury bonds, corporate bonds, tax-free bonds, or other types of bonds, because they have no hedge against inflation. You have to center your whole investment portfolio around stock ownership—not lending money. You have to be the owner of money (by owning stocks)—not the lender of money (by owning bonds)."

Throughout this entire century, conservative investors have been drawn to bonds because they are considered safer than stocks. But there's a huge price to pay for that safety. Generally speaking, the safer the investment, the lower the return. And the lower your return, the more purchasing power you lose.

"A dollar bill 20 years ago is now worth 37 cents in purchasing power," says Barry. "Postage stamps have gone from 13 cents to 32 cents. The average cost of an automobile 20 years ago was $5,700; now it's more than $19,000. A day in the hospital was $173; now it's $983. The name of the game is to grow money to offset the declining purchasing power of the dollar."

And the best way to grow money, says Barry, is to buy stocks. "Look at Microsoft," he explains. "A $10,000 investment in Microsoft ten years ago would now be worth more than $700,000 today. That's where the money is—equity ownership. You can become a partner with Bill Gates without ever asking his permission, simply by owning some shares of Microsoft stock."

If you invest regularly in stocks, says Barry, ultimately you'll make more from your investments than you do from your job. "There are only two kinds of money. There's people at work and there's money at work, and there's no question which is going to last longer. You're going to wear out, I'm going to wear out. We're finite commodities. But equity ownership—money—doesn't die, it doesn't become disabled, and it doesn't go on vacation, if it's handled reasonably well."

The following chart illustrates the dramatic difference in the long-term returns of stocks over bonds. While $1 invested in long-term U.S. government bonds in 1926 would have grown to about $35 in 1997, $1 invested in the broad stock market over the same period would have grown to about $1,650. Invested in smaller emerging growth stocks for the same period, that $1 would have grown to $5,700.

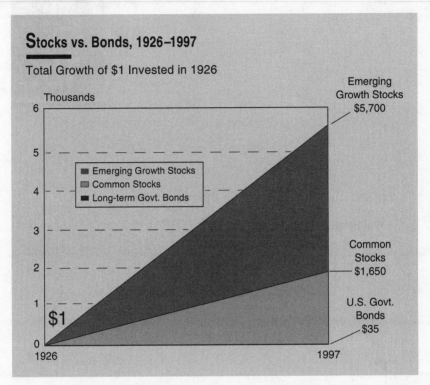

Stocks vs. Bonds, 1926–1997

Total Growth of $1 Invested in 1926

Thousands

Emerging
Growth Stocks
$5,700

- Emerging Growth Stocks
- Common Stocks
- Long-term Govt. Bonds

Common
Stocks
$1,650

U.S. Govt.
Bonds
$35

$1

1926   1997

16.

When you come to a fork in the road, take it.

—Yogi Berra

The straight and narrow is no place for investors. Diversification is the key to successful long-term investing. When you come to a fork in the road—and you have a decision between two stocks—go both ways. Buy some shares of each. Fill your portfolio with as broad a selection of stocks as you can afford.

Some investors think they're diversified when they own five or six stocks. But if some of those stocks are in the same industry group, that's not diversification. To be truly diversified, a portfolio needs several elements:

- Stocks from several different industry groups, such as foods, medical products, telecommunications, retail, manufacturing, chemicals, consumer goods, financial services, and computer goods (don't overstock your portfolio with the latest fad stocks)

- Large blue chip stocks as well as up-and-coming emerging growth stocks
- International mutual funds that help spread your assets to stock markets around the world

According to a long line of studies, the best approach to consistent, long-term performance is to spread your assets around. Next time you hit a fork in the road, go both ways.

17.

A study of economics usually reveals that the
best time to buy anything is last year.

—Marty Allen

There is a perception among some inexperienced investors that
the best days in the market are past, that stocks have gone as high as
they are going to go, and that it's too late to buy into the market.

Although there certainly is some truth to the notion that the best
time to buy anything was last year, that doesn't mean that prices won't
go even higher next year. In fact, stocks tend to go up most years, so
the price you'd pay for a stock today is likely to be higher than it would
have been a year ago. Which also means, of course, that by next year,
today's prices will probably look like a bargain. That's why smart
investors continue to add to their holdings year in and year out.

Those who are new to the market have a hard time grasping the
concept of an ever-rising market. They are under the notion that the law
of gravity should have some bearing on stock prices (what goes up

must come down, right?), and they're confounded as to how the market can continue to defy the laws of nature.

While the market does go through its share of ups and downs, generally speaking the trend is ever-upward. But there's nothing magical about it. The stock market's steady growth makes perfect sense. The price of a company's stock tends to go up as the value of the company goes up.

A company's value is determined by a range of factors such as its earnings, revenue, assets, cash position, debt-to-equity ratio, and other financial considerations. Most corporate managers devote their efforts to increasing the value of their company by increasing sales, earnings, and assets. The greater their sales, earnings, and assets, the more valuable their company becomes. That growing value is reflected in the rising price of its stock. The company is worth more, therefore the stock of the company is worth more. There's nothing magical or gravity-defying about it. Stock prices rise because the value of the companies they represent rises.

So if you missed this year's big run-up, don't despair. Put your money in the market and wait. Otherwise, you may be kicking yourself next year for missing out on such a great buying opportunity this year.

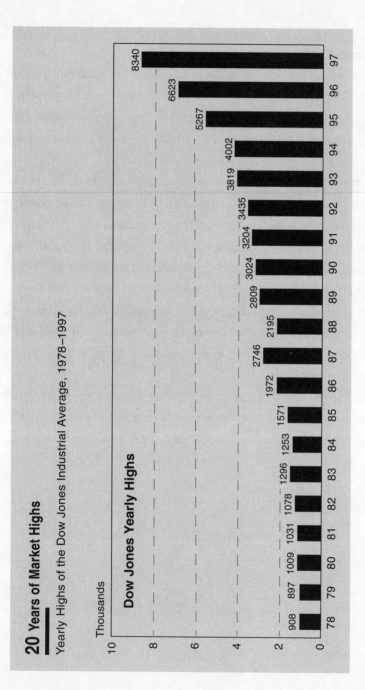

20 Years of Market Highs

Yearly Highs of the Dow Jones Industrial Average, 1978–1997

18.

I do not pretend to know what many ignorant
men are sure of.

—Clarence Darrow

I have a friend who is a financial planner. His modus operandi is to maneuver his clients' investment money through a broad universe of sector mutual funds, trying constantly to guess the right time to shift sectors or lighten the portfolio. He calls me sometimes to talk about an article he read or a speech he heard that spelled out in explicit, irrefutable terms why the market has gone as high as it's going to go, and is destined for a long, sobering correction. He was right in 1987, as he's pointed out now for more than a decade, but through most of the 1990s, he has often had his clients' money on the sidelines while the market pushed its way from one new high to another.

Although many investors try to time the market, none do it successfully with any consistency. In fact, the stock mutual funds that tend to do the best over the long term are the ones that remain almost fully invested in stocks all the time. Those fund managers have learned the futility of trying to figure out when the market is going to rise and fall.

"We don't do any market timing," says Todger Anderson, manager of the highly rated Westcore Midco Growth Fund. "There has never been any evidence that any money manager who uses market timing has been able to outperform the market over a number of cycles."

Aim Constellation Fund comanager Jonathan Schoolar adds, "We stay fully invested all the time. One bad decision can knock you out of the game. Any study will show you that the market makes the bulk of its moves in a very short time. If you miss it, you just can't make it up."

In 1995, after the Dow Jones Industrial Average had surged from about 3,800 to about 4,400, the manager of the Fidelity Magellan Fund decided that the market had gone high enough, and was headed for a correction. He sold out a large share of the fund's holdings—only to watch the market continue to climb to 5,000, then to 6,000, then to 7,000, and ultimately to 8,000, although by then, the fund manager had long since resigned from Magellan.

"You cannot time the market," insists investment manager James Barry. "You've got to be right two ways; you've got to be right getting in, and you've got to be right getting out. Most people do not have that capability—even the most respected investment professional in the business. You ask Peter Lynch, he'll tell you 'no.' You ask Michael Price, he'll tell you 'no.' You ask John Templeton, he'll tell you 'no.' You ask Warren Buffet, he'll tell you 'no.'"

"They do not try to time the market," adds Barry. "They buy quality stocks—quality merchandise—and they hold. If that quality merchandise drops in price, that's the Christmas card on-sale price. You buy more, if nothing has changed."

19.

Selling your winners and holding losers is like cutting your flowers and watering your weeds.

—Peter Lynch

Here's an all-too-common scenario of a novice investor: She buys six stocks. Three go up, three go down. She sells out the winners for a nice profit, and holds on to the losers in hopes that they rebound. With the profits from her winners, she pays her taxes and buys four more stocks. Two go up, two go down. She again sells the winners, keeps the losers, and repeats the process once more.

What she ultimately ends up with is a portfolio of losers. She has sold all the good stocks—paying taxes on the gains—and held on to the losers. If she had done the opposite, she would have a portfolio of winners and a nice tax break from dumping the losers. Your ultimate goal should be to accumulate a portfolio of great stocks. You don't do that by selling out your winners. Cut your losses and let your winners run.

20

Don't fight forces; use them.

—Buckminster Fuller

Never buy a stock on the way down. Never sell on the way up. Momentum is one of the strongest forces of the stock market. When stocks catch fire, they can climb far beyond reasonable levels. And when they drop, they can also drop beyond all common reason or expectations.

When you sell a stock on the way up—hoping to time your move at the peak—you risk missing out on even greater growth. Imagine investors who sold out their Wal-Mart stock in 1969 after a nice run-up. If they had held onto the stock instead, $1,000 worth of Wal-Mart stock would have grown to more than $1 million 25 years later.

When you try to time a buy on the way down—hoping to catch it at the bottom before it turns around—you could be in for a long unexpected drop. As Peter Lynch, former manager of the Fidelity Magellan Fund, once put it, "It's always darkest before pitch black." In the early

1990s, I followed Prime Motor Inns stock as it dropped from $35 to $13 a share, where I finally bought it, believing it had reached the bottom. It hadn't. It continued to drop to $10, $5, $3, $1, and into bankruptcy.

When you buy a fallen stock, try to be sure that the stock has hit the bottom, and has shown some evidence of a turnaround. Then ride the stock's upward momentum as long as the trend remains positive. As they say on Wall Street, "Don't fight the tape."

21.

A cynic is a man who, when he smells
flowers, looks around for a coffin.

—H.L. Mencken

If you follow the stock market, you're probably familiar with a certain breed of investment expert who thrives on the negative. The market is always too high, they say. The next free fall is just around the corner. Known in the business as "bears," they relish every down market.

But during the best of times—when the market is constantly cracking new highs—bears are simply inconsolable. The higher stocks climb, the harder they look for excuses to cast a negative spin on the market's good fortune.

In 1995, in the early stages of one of the nation's greatest bull markets, an investment newsletter writer was grousing over the booming market, and warning that today's investor wouldn't know how to handle a bear market. Then he offered this hypothetical example of a stock market investor's worst nightmare: "What happened to the 51-year-old who put all of his retirement fund in stocks during the wildly bullish year of 1968, to retire in 1982 (at the end of a long bear market)?" The investor's fate, said the writer, was a mere a 4.3 percent average annual return for the period.

Let's examine that a little closer: Even in this worst-case long-term scenario, putting all of his money in the market at the highest possible point, investing nothing else for the next 14 years, and pulling it all out at the lowest possible point—pure dumb luck combined with pure dumb investing—he would have still earned a 4.3 percent average annual *gain.*

And when you inject some common sense into this worst-case scenario, the returns become considerably more impressive.

For instance, let's assume that instead of putting all of his money into the market at one time in 1968, this 51-year-old investor had invested an equal amount each year throughout his final 14 working years, from 1968 to 1981. Then upon retiring in 1982, instead of selling all his stocks the day he retired, he took a common-sense approach, and sold just a portion of his stocks at a time over the next 14 years (through 1995).

As the following chart illustrates, that simple approach would have yielded a very respectable 13 percent average annual return. In dollar terms, if he had invested $10,000 a year from 1968 to 1981, his $140,000 investment would have produced a payout during his first 14 years of retirement of well over $700,000.

In fact, if he had kept all of that money in stocks (and lived on other means), by 1997 his $140,000 investment would have grown to a tidy $2.9 million—all despite investing during one of the most dismal bear markets of this century.

Stocks move in fits and starts. You can enjoy the bull markets a whole lot more—and smell the roses—if you've had the courage and conviction to invest during the bear markets.

The Benefits of Bear Market Investing

The following table shows the returns from investing $10,000 in stocks each year of the bear market from 1968 to 1981, then selling out those stocks over the next 14 years (1982–1995). In short, it shows the growth of $10,000 in 14 succeeding 14-year periods.

Year Invested	(Dow Average)	Year Sold Out	(Dow Average)	Average Annual Return (Including Dividends)	Total Invested	Total Returned
1968	(906)	1982	(884)	4.3	$ 10,000	$ 17,000
1969	(876)	1983	(1190)	7	10,000	22,600
1970	(753)	1984	(1178)	8	10,000	29,400
1971	(884)	1985	(1330)	7.7	10,000	28,000
1972	(949)	1986	(1797)	9.5	10,000	36,000
1973	(924)	1987	(2264)	12	10,000	49,000
1974	(759)	1988	(2062)	12.5	10,000	52,000
1975	(803)	1989	(2510)	13.5	10,000	59,000
1976	(975)	1990	(2670)	12.5	10,000	52,000
1977	(895)	1991	(2933)	14	10,000	63,000
1978	(820)	1992	(3282)	15.5	10,000	75,000
1979	(844)	1993	(3565)	15.5	10,000	75,000
1980	(891)	1994	(3735)	15.5	10,000	75,000
1981	(933)	1995	(5117)	18	10,000	101,000
Totals				13% (average)	$140,000	$734,000

Total invested: $140,000

Total returned: $734,000

Average annual compounded return: 13%

Total if all money was left in the market through 1995: $1.98 million

Total if all money was left in the market through 1997: $2.9 million

22.

Had there been a computer a hundred years ago, it would probably have predicted that by now there would be so many horse-drawn vehicles it would be impossible to clean up all the manure.

—K. William Kapp

The world of stock market analysis is generally divided into two broad camps—fundamental analysts, who look at the market on a stock-by-stock basis; and technical analysts, who focus on broad economic trends and recurring patterns to attempt to predict price movements in the market.

Both methods have their flaws, but most of the top-performing stock fund managers favor fundamental analysis. "We're buy-and-sell stock managers," says Fred Kobrick, manager of the highly ranked State Street Research Capital Fund. "We don't go by themes or trends. We go stock by stock."

The premise of fundamental analysis is that a stock's value depends on the company's present and future earnings. Also referred to as a "bottom-up" approach, fundamental analysis attempts to identify individual stocks that have exceptional earnings potential, or are undervalued relative to their earnings.

By contrast, the premise of technical analysis is that all the known information about a stock, industry, or national market is already reflected in the price of the stock, so rather than focus on individual stocks, technical analysts look at the big picture. Technical analysis—also known as a "top-down" approach—is not concerned with the financial strength of individual companies, but rather with the anticipated movement of the overall market.

Fundamental purists consider technical analysis to be a hit-and-miss approach—like all market-timing approaches—that can cost you big money in the long run. "One bad decision in the top-down style can knock you out of the game," says Jon Schoolar, co-manager of the Aim Constellation Fund. Rather than try to time the market with charts and graphs—and risk missing a big run-up in the market—Schoolar thinks it's better simply to stay fully invested all the time.

"Charts tell you what has happened—not what's going to happen," says Schoolar. "We don't put any stock at all in charts. In fact, I hate charts. I've never met a rich technician."

While Schoolar's sentiments mirror those of a lot of his colleagues in the profession, there are others like Paul H.Wick of the Seligman Communications and Information Fund who try to combine both disciplines. Wick looks at the economy and the most promising sectors, and then he looks for individual stocks that stand to benefit the most from those economic trends. As a result, says Wick, "I think we've done a good job of picking not only the right sectors, but the right stocks within those sectors."

23.

It's taken all of my life to understand that it is
not necessary to understand everything.

—Rene Coty

Serious investors tend to lose too much sleep fretting over exactly
when to buy into the market. No question, some periods are better than
others, but all in all, over the past 65 years there really never has been a
bad time to buy stocks for those with a long-term perspective.

In fact, even if you've failed miserably at timing your buying decisions, investing each year at the very peak of the market, chances are
you've still enjoyed surprisingly strong returns. What's even more surprising is the scant difference between your returns investing at the
peak, and the returns you would have earned had you invested each
year at the market low.

As the following chart demonstrates, the difference, in terms of total
return over the past 20 years, amounts to less than 1 percent per year!

The chart compares the returns from a portfolio in which all stocks
were purchased at the top of the market each year for a 20-year period

through 1996, versus a portfolio of stocks purchased at the bottom of the market each year for the same period. While clearly the best-case portfolio enjoyed the greater yield, both portfolios posted impressive returns.

Buying at the Market Peak versus the Market Low

20-Year Performance Investing $5,000 Annually at the Market High versus the Market Low (based on the Dow Jones Industrial Average).

	Worst-Case Portfolio Buying at the market high			Best-Case Portfolio Buying at the market low	
Month of Market High	Cumulative Investment	Portfolio Account Value on 12/31	Month of Market Low	Cumulative Investment	Portfolio Account Value on 12/31
1/77	$ 5,000	$ 4,587	11/77	$ 5,000	$ 5,089
9/78	10,000	9,447	2/78	10,000	10,986
10/79	15,000	15,669	11/79	15,000	17,329
11/80	20,000	24,067	4/80	20,000	27,336
4/81	25,000	27,803	9/81	25,000	31,593
12/82	30,000	40,340	8/82	30,000	46,123
11/83	35,000	55,804	1/83	35,000	64,227
1/84	40,000	61,756	7/84	40,000	70,640
12/85	45,000	87,473	1/85	45,000	100,625
12/86	50,000	116,182	1/86	50,000	134,155
8/87	55,000	126,246	10/87	55,000	146,411
10/88	60,000	152,367	1/88	60,000	175,787
10/89	65,000	206,575	1/89	65,000	238,498
7/90	70,000	210,081	10/90	70,000	242,607
12/91	75,000	265,895	2/91	75,000	306,962
6/92	80,000	290,645	10/92	80,000	334,857
8/93	85,000	345,084	4/93	85,000	397,164
8/94	90,000	367,517	11/94	90,000	422,428
12/95	95,000	507,898	1/95	95,000	584,861
11/96	100,000	659,369	1/96	100,000	759,672

Average Annual Rate of Return: 15.48%   **Average Annual Rate of Return: 16.35%**

Source: Towers Data Systems, Inc.

By the way, if you're looking for seasonal trends, you might notice that the best time to sell—when the market seems most likely to hit its high (see "Worst-Case" chart)—would apparently be in the fall and winter. Unfortunately, the best time to buy—when the market is most likely to hit its low (see "Best-Case" chart)—would also appear to be in the fall and winter. Just one more good reason not to worry about trying to time the market.

24

Don't put all your eggs in one basket.

—Old adage

If you have most of your money wrapped up in your company retirement plan, diversification could be a serious problem for you—depending on your company's plan. Many companies offer matching programs that allow investors to build up a large position in the company's stock. In some cases, the company even matches the employees' contributions share for share. Many investors have built a fortune by using those plans with a growing company. But they can also spell disaster if the company hits on hard times. A friend of mine was on such a plan when he worked for Cray Research, the company that pioneered the supercomputer.

Not only did my friend depend on Cray for his livelihood, but his entire retirement portfolio was tied up in Cray stock. When business began to wane at the company, not only did he lose his job, he saw his retirement holdings drop dramatically. The stock dropped from over

$100 a share to about $25 a share, at which point Cray was acquired by Silicon Graphics, and converted to Silicon Graphics stock. But the slide didn't end there. After the merger, Silicon Graphics stock dropped from about $30 per share to about $15, where it was trading in early 1998. My friend lost more than 80 percent of his retirement investments— and his job.

Employees at many other companies have had similar or even worse experiences, losing their jobs and their entire retirement savings when their companies folded. If your firm offers a matching-share stock purchase retirement plan, by all means put some of your money in that plan, but don't bet the farm. Make sure you have a diversified portfolio of other investments beyond the company stock.

25.

No one would ever have crossed the ocean if he could have gotten off the ship in the storm.

—Charles F. Kettering

If you want to succeed in the market, you need to ignore the short-term turbulence and focus on the long-term. If you sell out your holdings every time the market hits a snag, you will never enjoy success in the market. Remember, if you're investing for your retirement—and that retirement will be years from now—it doesn't matter how the market does today, this week, or even this year. Recognize that market volatility is a given. There will be down times in the market. When they come, don't jump ship. Those are buying opportunities—not selling opportunities. Focus on the long term, and stay on board. Over time, your ship *will* come in.

26.

Buy when the enemy is at your gate, and sell the minute you hear your cavalry's bugle sounding charge.

—Baron Rothschild

Sometimes a national or global crisis can cause stock prices across the board to plunge. Those times of crisis can make great buying opportunities. When Iraq invaded Kuwait in 1991, and the U.S. and its allies began making preparations to go to war, stock markets around the world began to drop. And they continued to drop until the day the allies began their attack. Once the assault began, however, and it looked as though the allies would make short work of the Iraqi army, the world's stock markets turned instantly from gloom to euphoria. The first day after the initial attack, the Dow Jones Industrial Average posted one of its biggest run-ups in history.

The next time a pending crisis sends stocks tumbling, remember that those with the courage to buy when the enemy is at the gate stand to gain the most when the bugle sounds its charge.

27

The beatings will continue until
morale improves.

—Anonymous

In the investment world, pessimism is always most rampant just before the market hits the bottom. When the stock market has been stagnant or falling for a long period, investors tend to get very discouraged and very down on the market.

Even the experts start questioning the market's potential. As one broker put it, "The sales resistance can be phenomenal. After a while, clients no longer want to hear that 'stocks don't ring a bell when they hit the bottom,' or that 'if they were a good value two months ago, they're a great buy now.' Those lines begin to lose some urgency, and investors start to tune out of the market."

When all seems hopeless, and prognosticators are predicting continued doom and gloom, get your money ready. The market is on the verge of bottoming out. When pessimism hits a peak, the next step is the dawn of optimism. And in the stock market, sometimes all it takes is a thin ray of hope to spark a long bull rally.

28.

Buy your straw hats in January and
your fur coats in July.

—Wall Street adage

Everyone likes a bargain, and it's common knowledge that the
savings are the greatest when no one is interested in buying. Snow skis
don't sell in the summer, and boats and swimwear go begging in the
fall. The same is true for the stock market. There are times when a specific sector of the economy may be out of favor on Wall Street—and
almost every industry goes through these cycles. In the late 1980s, it
was bank stocks; in the early 1990s, it was healthcare stocks. A good
time to build a position in a stock is when its industry is out of favor on
Wall Street, and prices are sagging.

There also is some evidence of seasonal patterns in the stock market, according to Princeton professor and market guru Burton Malkiel.
"Investigators have documented a January effect where stock returns are
abnormally higher during the first few days of January," he explains.

"There also seem to be day-of-the-week effects. For example, there is some justification for the expression 'Blue Monday' on Wall Street. The general problem with these anomalies, however, is that they are not dependable each year, and they are small relative to the transactions costs involved in trying to exploit them."

29.

Buy on weakness, sell on strength.

—Wall Street adage

Even good companies can go through a tough year or a tough quarter. And when they do, Wall Street punishes them—often mercilessly. A disappointing earnings report can cause the price of a stock to tumble far beyond what it should. Bad news about a company can also cause the stock price to drop. In 1994, when Intel reported that its Pentium chip was causing some mistakes in large calculations, its stock price dropped from about $65 a share to $56. But once the company resolved the problem, the stock not only moved back up to its original high, but continued to climb to $156 a share—a $100 gain (179 percent) in just seven months.

In 1996, America Online instituted a new unlimited use policy for customers willing to pay $19.95 per month. The response was so overwhelming the company couldn't meet demand. Seems like exactly the kind of problem most businesses would love, but Wall Street hammered the stock, knocking it from a high of $71 to a low of $25 in just two months. A year later, the stock had bounced back into the $70s, and investors smart enough to buy the stock in its time of trouble earned a return of more than 180 percent in just one year.

John W. Rogers, Jr., of the Ariel Funds, likes to buy stocks when no one else wants them. "We like to buy smaller and midsized companies when they're cheap and out of favor," he explains. "We look at the private market value of the companies. We look at discount of future cash flows of companies and what comparable companies are being sold at if someone's taking them over. When talking about private market value, we really are trying to get a sense of what a rational, informed buyer of the entire enterprise would pay for the company. The heart of the process is the cash flow. Typically, less than eight times cash flow is something we feel comfortable buying. That's the high end for us. If it is at six or seven times cash flow, that is clearly a better bargain."

Smart investors watch for those types of opportunities when the market pushes down the price of a stock because of a temporary problem that may have no bearing on the company's long-term prospects. That's when they swoop in and buy the stock to hold until the company rebounds.

30.

Buy on the rumor, sell on the news.

—Wall Street adage

If you follow the financial section of the newspaper, sometimes you'll see a headline to this effect: "ABC Corp. reports record earnings. Stock drops $1.50 per share."

Why is that? Why after reporting record profits would a stock drop in price?

There is a logical explanation—in its own illogical Wall Street kind of way. Traders in the market buy on rumors and speculation, not on news. They may hear well in advance that a company expects to report record earnings, so they begin to buy the stock, pushing up the price well before the company issues its earnings reports. By the time the earnings report is finally released to the public, the price of the stock already reflects that earnings increase.

Once the news is out, traders sell out their holdings, taking some profits to chase the next rumor. And by selling out the day of the new earnings report, they often cause a slight drop in the price of the stock.

The effect can be magnified if earnings come in lower than expected. If analysts expect an increase of 20 percent—driving up the price accordingly—and instead earnings rise just 10 percent, investors will drive the price back down. Wall Street does not like earnings "surprises" on the low side.

The reverse effect can also happen. Sometimes when a company reports a loss, the stock price goes up. Speculation over a disappointing earnings report can push a price down. By the time the news is released, the price may already be near rock bottom, so traders jump shortly after the bad news hits, to ride the price back up.

While short-term professional traders may profit on the rumor mill, most individual investors would have a hard time keeping up. It's hard to compete with full-time professionals, who are often in and out of a stock before the news reaches the general public.

31.

When you go to buy, use your eyes,
not your ears.

—Czechoslovakian proverb

Heard a hot tip on a stock? Can't wait to plunk down thousands of dollars to cash in? Look before you leap. Hot tips circulate constantly around Wall Street. Most are baseless. That's not to say ignore all the tips you hear, but before you buy, do a little research. Read about the company, dig through its annual report. Check out its product line. Take a look at its long-term earnings and revenue, and see if it's the kind of stock you want to have in your portfolio.

The one exception would be if your broker comes to you with a hot pick. If you have had good success in the past following your broker's recommendations, it's probably worth buying.

Otherwise, think of buying a stock in the same way you would think of buying a business. "Try to value the company's worth if it were sold," says Franklin Resources Fund Manager Michael Price. "What would somebody pay for the business?" You would never acquire a business based strictly on a hot tip. Do your homework. Then, if everything checks out, buy the stock. But buy it because it's a good company with solid long-term potential—not because your brother or your best friend gave you a hot tip on the stock.

32.

Fortune favors the bold.

—Terence, Roman playwright

To be a good investor takes persistence. To be a great investor takes courage. "The more gut-wrenching a decision, the bigger the potential for capital gains," says George Vanderheiden, manager of the Fidelity Advisor Growth Opportunities Fund.

Betting heavily in a down market or on a depressed sector takes a lot more daring than it would to put your money in a safe, secure money market account. The payoff can be breathtaking.

David Ellison, manager of the highly rated Fidelity Select Home Finance Portfolio, tries to keep investing and brace for the good times. In a specialty as fickle as bank and finance stocks, Ellison has learned that courage can pay big dividends.

"People are afraid of rising interest rates," he explains. "When rates go up, they start selling. That's when you want to be in the market.

You have to stay optimistic in this business. You have to always feel that things are going to turn around. You buy when fear is high—when people are anticipating the worst in respect to interest rates, and stocks are near their 52-week lows. One whiff of good news, and those stocks are all going to double."

Building a Winning Portfolio

PART

3

33.

Buy low, sell high.

—Wall Street battle cry

Whathat could be easier? Yet as elementary and logical as it may sound, buying low and selling high is much easier said than done—as many a new investor would attest. What makes the concept so difficult is that it clashes with every fiber of human impulse and emotion. When stocks are blazing through a strong bull rally, and every news show reports a new market high, it's hard to resist the impulse to jump in while the market's hot. Then, when stocks begin to go south and the economic outlook dims, emotion prods us to pull the plug and sell out before things get even worse. The result for the uninitiated is that they buy when stocks are pushing new highs, and sell when they sink to their lowest levels.

In truth, it takes nerves of steel to buy low and sell high, to put your money on the line when the market is floundering, and to sell out when everyone else is buying in. But that's what separates the winners from the losers, the rich from the rest. Only after you understand not only the psychology of the market, but also the history of the market, does it become easier to get it right. There will be fluctuations in stock prices, with high points and low points every year. Smart investors try to use those fluctuations to maximize their returns, bolstering their holdings when stocks are down, and lightening up their position when euphoria has driven up prices beyond reason. *Buy low, sell high.*

34.

The race is not always to the swift, nor the battle to the strong—but that's the way you have to bet.

—Damon Runyon

Some aggressive investment managers use momentum to time their buy and sell decisions. They load up on stocks with rapidly growing earnings, but they are quick to dump them if the earnings growth rate declines.

"We like to find stocks that have business momentum," says Christopher Boyd, comanager of the American Century Ultra Investors Fund. "We look for earnings and revenue acceleration. We're not as concerned about the size of the company as we are the momentum of the business. We're just trying to put the best growth companies in the portfolio."

But Boyd doesn't wait for the company's annual report to see whether it's in a growth spurt. "By then it's too late. We look at things like orders and backlog that may have an effect on future earnings reports."

While momentum can be an important consideration in buying a stock, falling momentum can be equally important in deciding when to sell.

"We emphasize the sell side," says Jon Schoolar, comanager of the Aim Constellation Fund. "Instead of sitting around talking about what to buy, we focus on what we should get rid of." Any stocks that show a declining earnings growth rate are quickly dropped from the fund.

In examining a company's earnings, Schoolar is more concerned about the present earnings than he is past earnings or future projections. "We don't try to project earnings; we follow earnings. We also don't try to project sales of a new product. We wait and see how it does, and then we may make future sales projections based on its initial market results. We just won't buy unsubstantiated stories. We want to be able to get our hands around something we can measure."

Schoolar considers growth momentum to be more important than the stock's price-earnings ratio. "We do look at price-earnings ratios," says Schoolar, "but we're not value investors. The main consideration with PEs is the higher the PE, the tighter our sell discipline. If a high PE stock shows any drop in momentum, we are much quicker to sell it."

Boyd agrees. "We're more interested in the direction and sustain-ability of the growth rate than in PEs and other value factors," he explains. "But we're always aware of the PE. A high PE stock that is starting to lose growth momentum can spell trouble."

35.

You have to sit back quietly and let the
bird walk in front of you before you shoot.

—James Crabbe, founder, Crabbe Huson Mutual Funds

James Crabbe looks for undervalued stocks that the market has punished or forgotten. "We try to use the emotion of the market as an opportunity to buy good companies at low prices," he says. "I've seen times when a single negative earnings report would cut the price of a stock by 50 percent." Those are the stocks that grab his interest. He may not invest in every stock that takes a hit, but he will take a close look to see if there's a chance it can rebound.

"We want to see if the company has done something to correct its problems," Crabbe explains. "We're not going to invest in that stock unless we've figured out why and how the company is going to bounce back. Maybe it's new management, maybe it's a new subsidiary, maybe it's a new product, or some cost-cutting measures. Only after we've figured that out will we buy the stock."

While Crabbe agrees in principle with the efficient market theory (which holds that Wall Street will ultimately value every stock correctly relative to every other stock), he believes there are windows of opportunity when prices are a bit out of whack. "Over the short term, emotions can cause the stock of a good company to drop further than it should." Disappointing earnings, a failed product launch, or other bad news can cause the market to overreact. That's when Crabbe makes his move.

"It's a lot like turkey hunting," he explains. "You have to be patient. You have to sit back quietly and let the bird walk in front of you before you shoot."

You just need to pull the trigger when the price is right.

36

Yellow cat, black cat, as long as it catches
mice, it's a good cat.

—Deng Xiaoping

Great stocks come in many different sizes and styles. Don't always look for the trendiest high-tech stocks. Some of the dullest companies can make great stocks. RPM, Inc., for instance, is in the business of manufacturing paints and coatings. Not glamorous stuff, but the company has posted 49 consecutive years of record earnings, while its stock price has moved up, on average, about 15 percent per year. Dull, yes, but profitable as well. Apple Computer, on the other hand, has always been considered a glamorous company on the leading edge of technology, but the stock has been disappointing for years.

"A lot of money has been lost in fad stocks, and a lot of money has been made in some very dull stocks," says Fidelity Fund Manager George Vanderheiden.

"We focus on consistent industries," says Ariel Funds Manager John W. Rogers, Jr. "We don't buy a little bit of everything to make sure we have all our industries covered. We really want to work on the industries that have the most predictable earnings streams. Over the years, you would not see us owning the high-technology companies, because they're very volatile, very unpredictable. You won't see us owning the commodity-oriented companies like gold and silver, oil and gas, either. And you won't see us owning the heavy cyclical companies—big autos, machine tools, heavy manufacturing. We really don't invest in those kinds of businesses.

"The kinds of companies we invest in would be household goods like the ones you see in your grocery store," adds Rogers. "But not big companies like Procter & Gamble. We concentrate on small to mid-sized companies like Clorox, First Brand (Glad garbage bags), McCormack Spice Company, Herman Miller, General Binding, and American Media (which owns the *National Enquirer).*

"These companies generate positive cash flow, have high returns on assets and equity, and have a strong brand name in their specific industry niche," explains Rogers. "When it comes to bleach, you think of Clorox. When it comes to tabloid journalism, you think of the *National Enquirer.* That's the same way Warren Buffett talks about Gillette and Coca-Cola—big companies with strong brand names. We're buying brand names in the smaller and medium-sized sector."

Look for good stocks—not just glamorous companies.

37

Don't buy the house, buy the neighborhood.

—Anonymous

If you want to make big money in the stock market, figure out which sectors are growing the fastest, and put some money in them.

It isn't difficult to recognize which area has the most potential for growth over the next few decades. It's technology—computers, medical products, and telecommunications. If you don't have any investments in up-and-coming technology companies, then you could be missing out on some big gains in your portfolio. "For many years, technology was the federal government flying us to the moon," explains Boca Raton–based money manager Jim Barry. "Now technology is in the private sector. A few years back, to buy a portable phone, you had to pay about $3,000. And it had a battery in it that was so big you could hardly carry it around. Now they're giving phones away as premiums because technology has brought the cost of phones down so much that the whole world can now afford portable phones."

Adds William Berger of the Berger Funds, "We're seeing some of these small companies growing at clips of 50 percent or more a year. Technology is the area that seems to have the best growth possibilities in this country. That's the area we can prevail in in the global market. We will continue to lead the world through new advancements in technology."

You can reap the rewards of the technology boom by packing your portfolio with some of the top performing stocks of the computer, medical, and telecommunications industries.

38.

Put your eggs in one basket and—
WATCH THAT BASKET.

—Mark Twain, *Pudd'nhead Wilson*

Some professional investors specialize in a specific sector of the market, and their astute moves in that area of the market net them some big returns. But for most investors, that's a strategy to avoid. There are times, however, when it can be profitable to specialize in one stock (as long as you maintain a diversified portfolio of other stocks as well). Some stocks are known as "bouncers" because their prices bounce up and down in a fairly predictable pattern. Although those stocks may not necessarily do well over the long term, they can net short-term traders big gains on the swings.

I used to play the bounce on a stock called Network Systems. It had a fairly consistent pattern of moving from about $15 to $25 and back to $15. When it dropped to near $16, I would buy; when it rose to near $25, I would sell. Even though it ultimately dropped to about $10 a

share—well below the price of the stock when I first started buying it—
I still came out way ahead of the game by playing the bounce.

If you come across a bouncer, take some fun money and practice
playing the bounce. Many small investors focus almost exclusively on
playing bouncers, often with exceptional results.

39.

Where there's smoke, there's panic.

—Richard Jeni

As uncertain as stock investing may seem, there are still many certainties in the market. One such certainty is that no matter how robust the economy or the market may seem, the next correction is always just around the corner. This is not the warning of a perpetual pessimist. It is simply a fact of the stock market.

A *correction,* for those unfamiliar with the term, is a euphemism for a substantial drop in stock prices—the logic of the term being that when the market gets too high, it "corrects" itself by falling in value. There's a fine line between a correction and a crash, but one might consider a market decline of 5 to 20 percent to be a correction, and more than 20 percent to be a crash.

Throughout the past century there have been hundreds of market corrections. They typically occur several times a year. And whenever they do, the press and the TV talk shows always treat the occasion like the second coming of 1929. They talk in dire terms, quoting the experts on the possible consequences of this unexpected bombshell, and striking fear into the hearts of novice investors.

But the investment veterans know that corrections are no reason for panic. They aren't even news. They are just a natural part of the stock market process. But the media frenzy that accompanies the more severe corrections tends to spook some inexperienced investors into selling their holdings—in classic "buy high, sell low" fashion. Experienced investors know better. They wait patiently for these corrections, and coolly add to their holdings when they come, loading up while prices are at a discount.

In the stock market, there's often smoke, but seldom fire. Focus on the long term when the market drops, and shop around for some good buys on quality stocks. Where there's smoke, there are bargains.

40

We try to buy panic and sell euphoria.

—Paul H. Wick, manager, Seligman Communications and Information Fund

"There's always a lot of volatility with small stocks," says Paul H. Wick, fund manager of the high-flying Seligman Communications and Information Fund. "We just try to recognize the buying opportunities."

Like many other aggressive fund managers, Wick is momentum-oriented. He looks for stocks with rapid earnings growth in the range of 30 to 60 percent per year. He also likes companies with a lot of cash flow and profit margins of 18 percent or more. "Some technology products can hit a sweet spot in the market and really grow at astronomical rates for a while. But their big success usually doesn't last too long." When the growth begins to ebb, Wick sells.

He also sells when the stock or its sector gets too high. "When the public gets too enthusiastic about a sector, we'll often sell out and move into something else."

While Wick likes to "buy panic and sell euphoria," he tries to keep his own emotions out of the decision-making process. Instead he relies on facts and figures. "We get to know the companies well. I've probably visited 70 percent of the companies in our portfolio. By knowing a company well, we can take advantage of the volatility in the market. We can recognize buying opportunities and build a position in the stock when it's at a low moment."

Wick uses that same attention to detail to time his selling decisions. He also looks for any type of bad news or earnings disappointments that could affect the stock. When he sees it, he acts quickly. "One thing that has really helped the fund's performance the past few years is that we've gotten better at cutting our losses quickly before they become big losses," he says.

41.

I am easily satisfied with the very best.

—Winston Churchill

How do you build an all-star portfolio? You do it, in part, by focusing on stocks that have done well for many years.

That's the approach I use in selecting the stocks for the book, *The 100 Best Stocks to Own in America* (now in its 5th edition; Dearborn Financial Publishing, 1998). How successful has that approach been over the years? If you had invested in the number one–rated stock in each of the five editions of the book (Anheuser-Busch in 1989, Philip Morris in 1991, William Wrigley in 1993, Gillette in 1995, and Medtronic in 1997), through 1997, you would have enjoyed a graduated total return of 165 percent—considerably better than the 144 percent market average for the same period. (See chart.)

What do I look for in selecting stocks for *The 100 Best Stocks*? The first criterion is consistency. The companies I like best are those that tend to post record earnings and revenue year in and year out. While it is true that strong past performance is no guarantee of future success, it's difficult to ignore the success of companies such as RPM, a paints and chemicals manufacturer that has posted nearly 50 consecutive years of record earnings, and Automatic Data Processing (ADP), a computer services company that specializes in processing payroll checks, which also has posted nearly 50 consecutive years of record sales and earnings.

What does a stellar track record tell you about a company? Obviously it doesn't tell you that the company will enjoy another 50 straight years of record earnings. But it does indicate that the company is probably very well managed, that it is in a strong financial position, and that its products or services have found a very lucrative niche in the market. All other things being equal, there's a very high comfort level investing in a company that's grown every year for half a century.

Once I've identified the most consistent companies, I look at how fast that growth has come. For instance, I would favor a company that's posted earnings gains of 15 to 20 percent per year for the past ten years over one that's grown at 5 to 10 percent per year. Genuine Parts, an Atlanta-based auto parts retailer, has had nearly 40 straight years of record earnings and nearly 50 straight years of record sales, but the growth has been very slow from year to year. Not to detract from Genuine Parts—it's been in all five editions of *The 100 Best Stocks,* and it would be a rock-solid addition to any portfolio—but its earnings only tend to go up about 10 percent per year, and so does its stock price. I would give a higher rating to a company with a similar record of consistency but with a higher percentage of annual average earnings growth.

Finally, for companies that pay dividends, I like to see them raise those dividends every year. Not only is the rising dividend an added bonus for shareholders, it's also a sign of stability and optimism by the company.

As elementary as this stock selection system may seem, sometimes simplicity can be very effective.

How Top Picks Have Fared versus the Market

This chart compares the growth of the number one–ranked stock in each of the five editions of *The 100 Best Stocks to Own in America* versus the growth of the Dow Jones Industrial Average. It assumes a $10,000 investment in each of the five stocks the year they were ranked number one, versus an equal investment in the Dow Average each of those same five years. As the chart demonstrates, the five stocks outperformed the Dow during the period, 165 percent versus 144 percent.

| | | | | | Current Value | |
| | | | Total Return (12/97) | Dow Growth (12/97) | | |
Investment	Year	#1 pick			Stock	Dow
$10,000	1989	Anheuser-Busch	235%	261%	$33,500	$36,100
10,000	1991	Philip Morris	225	197	32,500	29,700
10,000	1993	William Wrigley	163	137	26,300	23,700
10,000	1995	Gillette	154	104	25,400	20,400
10,000	1997	Medtronic	48	21	14,800	12,100

Total Investment: $50,000

	Stock	Dow
Total value:	$132,500	$122,000
Total return:	165%	144%

42.

When it is not necessary to make a decision,
it is necessary not to make a decision.

—Lord Falkland

Over the past decade, *The 100 Best Stocks to Own in America* has become a popular handbook not just for investors but for brokers, as well, who use the book to come up with some good blue chip stocks to recommend to their clients.

But frequently, I run into Wall Street professionals who snidely question how a book that comes out every two years could possibly be of any value to investors. Some have even gone so far as to suggest that to serve its purpose, the book would need to be updated every month.

It's a suggestion I greet with cynical bemusement, usually pointing out that it wouldn't serve the readers' best interests to feature stocks that need to be bought and sold every month. The object is to find stocks that will provide good returns for years to come. It's a concept some money managers have a difficult time grasping. When you spend your whole life buying and selling stocks to try to get an edge on the market, it can be hard to admit that your clients might be better served if you did nothing at all. For the record, a portfolio of the 100 stocks in the very first edition of *The 100 Best Stocks* (published in 1989), would have outperformed well over 80 percent of all mutual funds over the next nine years. And that's without ever trading a single stock in the portfolio. Clearly, the long-term buy-and-hold approach is superior to most of the short-term, buy-and-sell games employed by the portfolio managers on Wall Street.

"In our society, long-term is breakfast time tomorrow morning," says investment adviser James Barry, Jr. "Instant gratification, instant pudding, instant lotteries. That is not how you make money investing. You have to think long-term."

With quality blue chip stocks, the object should be to accumulate—not buy and sell.

"You have to approach any selling decisions realizing that more than half the time you're inclined to sell, you would be better off holding than selling," says Mark Hulbert, publisher of the *Hulbert Financial Digest,* which rates investment newsletters. "Look at the crash of 1987. A lot of people sold right after the crash, and missed out on a 23 percent gain in the market in the following months. So you better make sure there's a preponderance of evidence in your favor before you sell."

43.

See everything; overlook a great deal;
correct a little.

—Pope John XXIII

Once you've established a portfolio of all-star stocks, it's probably a good idea to review the portfolio periodically, but there's no need to make wholesale changes. Minor adjustments—selling a few shares here, adding a few shares there—would not only be a more prudent approach, but also a more profitable one.

The Mairs and Power Growth Fund, which was started in 1958, has been one of the top performing mutual funds for many years while maintaining one of the lowest portfolio turnover ratios in the industry. Fund manager George Mairs III likes to find good quality stocks and stick with them.

"Our approach is to identify companies that we like and then to acquire shares in those companies at times when the stocks appear to provide good value," explains Mairs. "We have a master list of about 50 names—companies that we are quite familiar with—and we buy shares of those stocks at times when they appear to provide good value, and we'll lighten up on a position when they appear to us to be fully priced on a relative basis. We rarely ever eliminate a name from the portfolio. Most of our buying and selling is within that select group of names. In many cases, we will trim back a position that we think has outperformed the market and add to positions that have underperformed."

Rather than spend his time and resources scouring the market for new stocks to buy, Mairs is able to spend more time tracking his own small universe of 50 stocks to determine the best buy and sell price levels. "Our tendency is to buy stocks on dips rather than when they're making new highs. We tend to want to buy on bad news. There is a tendency on the part of many investors to be momentum players. They buy stocks simply because they are going up or are being highly touted. That tends to make those stocks overpriced. Our philosophy is the opposite," adds Mairs. "Once we've identified the stocks that we like, when those stocks get hammered—or simply lag the market—we add to those positions."

Most of the selling in the portfolio is aimed at freeing up money to use on other stocks. "Typically, we do a certain amount of trimming back in positions simply so that we have funds available to add to some of the things that are undervalued," says Mairs.

While some of the most aggressive stock funds have annual portfolio turnover ratios as high as 200 to 300 percent, the Mairs and Power Growth Fund turnover ratio is often less than 10 percent per year. "Those other funds are chasing stocks on a momentum basis," says Mairs, "and often you can get whipsawed [be on the wrong side of a transaction during a volatile market] doing that. They would never think of owning a stock like Supervalu where they might have to wait a year for the stock to move. They're too short term oriented. If a stock isn't moving, they want to get out of it. But they are ignoring the valuation underpinnings that we think are very important. Certainly there are periods when the momentum funds do well, but over the long-term, they don't seem to do that well. I think our buy-and-hold strategy—with some trimming and adjusting—makes a lot more sense."

Not only does it make sense for the long-term performance of the fund, but it also costs its shareholders a lot less in taxes. "We recognize that the taxable shareholder is penalized by the high trading, because high trading results in a lot of taxable gains," says Mairs. "We don't want to saddle these people with taxable gains unless we feel we can improve the performance of the fund."

Mairs does not try to time the market, generally keeping more than 90 percent of the fund's assets in stocks.

44

I want to buy stocks that no one else knows
about, and I want to sell them after everyone
discovers them.

—John Markese

"Our philosophy is very simple," says John Markese, president of the American Association of Individual Investors. "If you are
going to spend the time to analyze stocks and to understand the industry
and the products and the firm, your rewards will be much greater,
potentially, in stocks that aren't followed by the analyst community.
Why not operate in an area where you have a competitive advantage?
And then when Wall Street discovers your stocks, you take your profits
and go find some other undiscovered stocks."

In evaluating stocks, Markese looks at some very fundamental
factors. "I like to look at growth rates of sales and earnings, and I look
over a five-year period at the stability and pattern of the growth."

To determine whether a company is in the early stages of its growth curve, Markese looks at several factors:

- *Industry.* Is the company in a growing industry with strong long-term potential?
- *Position within the industry.* Does the company have a strong niche position within the industry?
- *Product line.* Is the company expanding its product line? Is it spending a good share of its revenue on research and development? Do its key products have solid long-term potential?
- *Profit margin.* The higher a stock's profit margin relative to the industry profit margin, the more attractive the stock. A high or growth profit margin is an indication that a company might still be in the early stage of its growth curve.
- *Rising PE.* "With a smaller growth company, I prefer to see a rising PE," says Markese. "Even though you're paying more for it, it indicates that the market is becoming aware of the potential growth of this firm. Stock price momentum is not a bad indicator of the beginnings of recognition. I don't want to buy a stock that has fallen off its high. I want a stock that is still being bought and discovered."
- *Relative strength.* "I'd like to look at the strength of the stock relative to the market and to its industry."
- *Management ownership.* Markese likes companies in which the management owns a significant share of the stock. He considers 30 to 40 percent ownership by management to be healthy, but would steer away from a company that had 70 percent or more ownership because of liquidity concerns. "Then it's almost like buying a minority interest in a private firm."

Markese recommends that investors buy small stocks with the intention of holding them for four or five years. On the other hand, he adds, "I would sell at any time that a significant piece of information about the firm came out that would change your view. That could be anything from a product change to a change in the industry to a technological change to a change in legislation. But as long as the company is continuing to do what it was doing when I bought the stock, I would hold on to it."

45

In the long run, it's earnings growth
that drives the stock.

—Roger Stamper

"People try to make a lot out of managing money, but it's really very simple," says Roger Stamper, manager of the highly rated Parkstone Small Capitalization Fund. "In the long run, it's earnings growth that drives the stock. When the market is topsy-turvy, when everyone is pessimistic, we still focus on the same factor—earnings. If earnings keep going up, then eventually the stock has to follow. The earnings will always bail you out."

Stamper likes small stocks with sustainable growth, although that can be difficult to determine. "You really can't quantify it. You want strong management, increasing market share, strong revenue growth, good products—all the intangibles that give you confidence the company is likely to grow."

Stamper is more likely to invest in companies he understands. "If I can paint a picture in my mind of what the company does and why its sales and earnings will continue to grow, that's a big plus for me." But Stamper is quick to bail out if the company begins to change its key strategies, or if earnings suddenly take a turn for the worse.

46.

The world pays for results.

—Gary Pilgrim

As portfolio manager of the PBHG Growth Fund, one of the nation's top performing mutual funds, Gary Pilgrim goes through all the usual screens to select stocks for his fund. But in the end, it is fast growth that really grabs his attention. "Twenty-five years in this business has taught me that a good company is a company that is doing good. The world pays for results."

Pilgrim grades stocks on a wide range of factors:

- *Strong growth.* He wants stocks with earnings and sales growth of at least 20 percent per year.
- *Sequential acceleration.* He likes stocks with increasing sales growth rates.
- *Earnings surprises.* He is drawn to companies that surprise the analysts by continuing to post higher-than-expected earnings.

- *Estimate revisions.* Similar to earnings surprises, Pilgrim likes companies that grow faster each year than analysts project.

When a company's growth momentum begins to slide, he unloads the stock.

"What we try to do is identify and hold on to the really high-growth stocks as long as it makes sense to do so. We'd like to hold them for four or five years, but that's pretty rare. Most growth companies go through stages of very rapid growth and then, for various reasons, they slow down. That growth phase may be nine months, or it may be three years. When they start to slow down, that's when we weed them out of the portfolio."

47.

Everything comes to him who hustles
while he waits.

—Thomas A. Edison

Like any other pursuit, the more you put into investing, the more
you will get out of it. Even when you're fully invested, it pays to continue to scout the market for stock prospects you could add to your
portfolio when more money becomes available.

That means not only finding good companies with solid financial
track records, but also tracking those stocks to see what type of PE
ratios they can support, and to figure out each stock's typical trading
range. That way, when money does become available, you'll have a
better idea of exactly when to buy the stock.

PBHG Growth Fund manager Gary Pilgrim only holds about 80 to
100 stocks at a time, but he keeps tabs on a universe of about 450
stocks, tracking and grading them on an ongoing basis. Of those 450
stocks, he uses a variety of screens to narrow the list to about 150 favorite stocks. When one of the 75 to 100 stocks in his portfolio begins to

ebb, he reaches into his reserve of stock candidates and picks a new stock that shows the most promise.

"The art form of this process is your continuous awareness of how a company is doing," says Pilgrim. "It's an ongoing process."

By continuing to follow the progress not only of the stocks in your own portfolio, but also of some stocks you may want to add, you'll give yourself a better chance of keeping your portfolio growing.

48.

Too much of a good thing is wonderful.

—Mae West

One of the most common issues facing investors is when to sell a stock. Investors are constantly looking for exactly the right moment.

But ideally, the perfect time to sell a good stock is never. If a company continues to maintain strong financial performance, increasing its earnings and revenue year in and year out, why sell? That's exactly the kind of stock you want to own.

There are a number of great blue chip stocks that have continued to perform well for many, many years, like Coca-Cola, Kellogg, and Merck. There has never been a good time to sell those stocks.

One of the biggest advantages of stock ownership is that you pay no taxes on your gains until you sell the stock. So if you hold a stock for life—or for many, many years—the stock can grow five-, ten-, 20-fold, or more, and you still pay no taxes on the gains (until you sell).

You also pay no commissions to sell and no commissions to reinvest in another stock. So your bias should be toward holding good stocks for the long term.

If a great company has a bad year or a bad quarter, then you should watch it carefully to make sure that the slide was temporary. In many cases, great companies are able to rebound quickly from a down year, and impatient investors who sell out too soon miss out on a big resurgence in the stock price. But if the company's financials continue to weaken in the second year, you may be justified to lighten your load or sell out entirely—even if the stock price has already dropped significantly. That's part of the game. But it's better to take a loss and move on to something with more promise than to stick with a stagnant or declining stock in hopes that it will go back up. At some point, it probably will rebound, but it could be a long time coming.

A lot of once-great stocks that hit the wall have taken years to recover. IBM was a great stock in the 1960s and 1970s, but it went through a decade and a half of subpar performance before finally rebounding in the mid-1990s. The Limited, WMX Technology (formerly Waste Management), Rubbermaid, Tyson Foods, Quaker Oats, and Gannett are all examples of once-great stocks that fizzled after years of strong performance.

But, with few exceptions, if your stocks continue to post strong financial returns, just hold on. Those are exactly the companies you want in your all-star portfolio.

49.

Nobody has ever bet enough on
a winning horse.

—Anonymous

In horse racing, when the bell sounds, your bet had better be in. You can't change it and you can't add to it. But in the stock market, if your horse starts strong, you can always go back to the table and bet some more.

"I take a farm system approach," says Fred Kobrick, portfolio manager of the fast-rising State Street Research Capital Fund. "If I find a stock that looks interesting, I'll buy a small position in it and watch it to see how the management operates. I'll weed out the ones that don't work out, and buy more of the good ones."

Even after a large run-up in the price, Kobrick may keep buying. In fact, it may even take a large move in the stock to convince him to buy more. When computer networking manufacturer Cisco Systems went public at $1.63 a share, Kobrick bought a small position and followed the progress of the company. The stock quickly rose to $3 a share. "We thought the management team executed so well that they actually lengthened their lead over their competition. That's when we knew it was a great company. We increased our position substantially." The stock has since grown more than 30-fold (including splits).

A few years earlier, Kobrick bought the stock of Chrysler Corp. at $10 a share. When the stock doubled to $20, he had dinner with Lee Iacocca and one of his chief managers. "From that discussion, I felt they were still executing well, so we made it the largest position in the fund. It went from $20 to $55 a share."

Next time one of your picks does well, don't kick yourself for not investing more. Be happy with your gains and reevaluate the strength of the company; if it still looks good, you can always bet more.

50

Luck is being ready for the chance.

—James Frank Dobie

By understanding the economic cycles and the effects they have on stocks, you may be able to get a step up on the market. Certain types of investments tend to do better during specific stages of the economy. You wouldn't want to make all your buying decisions based on the economic cycles, but you might improve your performance by shifting the weighting of your portfolio as the economy shifts.

Following are the five phases of a typical business cycle, and the types of investments that tend to perform the best in each cycle:

1. *Recession.* Characterized by falling production, peaking inflation, and weakened consumer confidence, recessions are usually a good time to buy cyclical stocks (such as automakers, paper companies, and other heavy manufacturers). Their earnings may look anemic, and their stock prices may be flounder-

ing, but they are among the first stocks to take off when the economy turns around. Long-term bonds are also a good bet in a recession, because the government tends to lower interest rates to help spur the economy. As interest rates go down, bond prices go up.

2. *Recovery.* Marked by stimulatory economic policies, falling inflation, and increasing consumer confidence, recovery is a good time to buy stocks, long-term bonds, precious metals, and commodities. Smaller emerging growth stocks may do especially well during a recovery, and cyclical stocks should still have some growth left. Real estate is also a good bet.

3. *Early upswing.* The recovery period is past, confidence is up, and the economy is gaining some momentum. This is the healthiest period of the cycle in a sense, because economic growth can continue without any signs of overheating or sharply higher inflation. Consumers are prepared to borrow and spend more, and businesses—facing increased capacity use—begin investing in plant or office expansion. Unemployment falls, but inflation may pick up. Higher operating levels allow many businesses to cut unit costs and increase margins and profits. The stock market should remain strong, while commodities will continue to rise modestly. The early upswing stage could last for several years. Real estate should continue to do well. Unload the cyclical stocks, whose growth is probably over.

4. *Late upswing.* The economic boom is in full swing. Manufacturing capacity utilization nears a peak—prompting an investment rally—and unemployment continues to fall. Property prices and rents move up strongly, prompting a construction boom. Inflation picks up as wages increase in the wake of labor shortages. With interest rates rising, bonds and bank stocks become less attractive. In fact, the overall stock market may hit a lull. But

commodity prices should continue to rise, bolstered by a huge demand for raw goods to feed the boom in manufacturing.

5. *Economic slowdown.* The economy begins to decline. Short-term interest rates move up sharply, peaking as confidence drops. The slowdown is exacerbated by the inventory correction as companies, suddenly fearing recession, try to reduce their inventory levels. Manufacturing capacity utilization begins to drop while wages continue to rise, resulting in increasing inflation. In the markets, bond yields top out and start to fall. The stock market may fall, perhaps significantly, with interest-sensitive stocks such as utilities faring the best. Commodity prices may also begin to decline. Long-term bonds, which rise as interest rates drop, may be your best investment.

51.

As people grow older, they often confuse
being careful with being wise.

—Anonymous

One of the biggest mistakes people of retirement age make is
that they simply don't expect to live to a ripe old age. They become too
conservative with their investments, taking a short-term approach
instead of planning for the long term. The fact is, even after you retire
you may be on this earth for another 20 to 30 years. If all of your money
is in conservative investments, your buying power will be slowly eroded
by inflation.

Often, people of retirement age will begin to pull their money out
of stocks and stock mutual funds and put them into CDs, bonds, and
U.S. Treasury bills. These income-bearing investments may pay decent
interest rates in the short term, but they provide no long-term appreciation. And, unlike a typical stock dividend that tends to rise with inflation, bonds and CD payments do not increase.

For example, let's compare the income stream from ten years of dividends from a typical blue chip company (Abbott Laboratories, for example) with an income stream from a ten-year certificate of deposit. To set the stage, let's say you bought a $10,000 CD in 1988, and, at the same time, bought $10,000 worth of Abbott Labs stock.

At its January 1, 1988, trading price of $12 (split-adjusted), you could have purchased 833 shares of Abbott Labs stock. In 1988, the stock paid a dividend of 30 cents. Multiply that by 833 shares, and your payout would have been $250 (2.5 percent).

At the same time, CDs were paying about 5 percent, which means your payout would have been $500 a year. It remained at $500 per year every year for the next ten years.

But while the Abbott dividend started out at just half the payout of the CD ($250 versus $500), the company steadily increased the dividend year in and year out. It had climbed from 30 cents to 50 cents by 1991, to 76 cents by 1994, and to $1.08 by 1997. That means, with 833 shares, your annual dividend would have been $900—a full $400 more than the CD was paying. (Based on your initial $10,000 investment, your $900 dividend would have been the equivalent of a 9 percent yield.)

So, strictly on dividend growth alone, you can see that it pays to invest in good blue chip stocks over "safe and secure" certificates of deposit and similar types of interest-bearing investments. In the long run, you'll receive a better income stream from dividend-paying stocks than you will with interest-bearing investments.

The other factor worth noting is capital appreciation. While stock price appreciation can vary significantly from stock to stock, over time the vast majority of blue chip stocks do provide excellent appreciation. Abbott Labs stock grew in price from $12 in 1988 to $65.50 at the close of 1997. In other words, while your $10,000 CD remained at $10,000 after ten years, your Abbott Labs stock would have climbed in value from $10,000 to $54,562.

So, dividend-paying blue chip stocks can give you the best of both worlds—an increasing stream of income and appreciation of capital. You may experience some short-term volatility with stocks, but your long-term returns will dramatically outpace the returns of a bond-based or CD-based portfolio, and your buying power will remain strong for years to come.

52.

All animals are equal, but some animals
are more equal than others.

—George Orwell, *Animal Farm*

You're already familiar with the "efficient market theory," which states essentially that all stocks are appropriately priced relative to each other at all times. In fact, that's the whole basis of the assertion that a chimp throwing darts could do just as well as an investment professional picking stocks through research and educated deduction.

But if you examine the track history of some of the more prominent stocks on the market, it would appear, in fact, that the market really isn't perfectly efficient—that some stocks are indeed "more equal" than others. That's one reason why some money managers are able to consistently outperform their peers. They're able to steer away from the perennial losers and invest in the stocks that tend to show more promise over the long term.

For instance, investors have continued to buy shares of companies such as General Motors and International Harvester (now Navistar

International), which have consistently underperformed the market for years, rather than to buy stocks of companies that tend to rise with the market, such as Gillette, Merck, and Johnson & Johnson.

Let's look at General Motors. Investors own more than $40 billion in General Motors stock. Brokers and analysts continue to recommend it to their clients—and investors continue to buy it—despite the fact that the company (and the stock) has been spinning its wheels for many years. General Motors stock was trading near $60 a share in late 1997—only $10 higher than its high of $50 in 1989. During that same period, the overall market tripled. In terms of earnings, the company actually made more money in 1989 ($6.34 per share) than it did in 1996 ($6.07 per share)—with many years of losses in between. The returns are not surprising, considering the intense global competition in the auto industry. With the increased manufacturing capacity of Asian carmakers, there is a glut of new automobiles on the international market, and the situation is not likely to change any time soon. It has been a consistent trend for 30 years. So why do brokers and analysts continue to recommend GM? Part of the attraction may be the fact that many investors drive GM cars, and they want to own a piece of the company. Unfortunately, that's a poor reason to buy a stock.

There's no question, GM or Navistar International or any of the other perennial market dogs could turn it around. It does happen from time to time. After a long period of poor performance, both Xerox Corp. and IBM turned the corner and began moving back up. But, as an investor, why take the chance? Instead, you should look for growing companies with solid track records, and avoid the slow-moving dinosaurs.

Check your portfolio for stocks that may have seen better days. "If you feel a company has lost its way, lost its focus, or lost its energy, that may be a time to sell," says Ariel Fund's John W. Rogers, Jr. "Does it still have that fire in the belly? You also have to understand the competitive landscape. Things can change. New competitors can come into an industry and cause problems for a company. You really need to be on top of that."

Some stocks are more equal than others. Successful investing requires not only the ability to identify the potential winners, but, just as important, to avoid the perennial losers. Before you buy a stock, make sure it's a company's that's on the upswing rather than one that's holding on for dear life.

53.

Stocks fall faster than they rise.

—Wall Street adage

While it's often good to buy stocks when they're down, it can be a mistake to jump on board too soon. When a stock takes a hit after a disappointing earnings report or some bad news from the company, bargain hunters are often quick to buy into the stock before the market pushes the price back up. In most cases, however, there is no need to hurry. Stocks really do tend to fall much faster than they rise. If the market has had a major correction, or a stock you follow has had a sudden free fall, be patient. Wait for the stock (or the market) to begin showing some upward momentum. You may not get in right at the bottom, but you can avoid buying into a falling star in mid fall.

In 1987, when the market dropped about 25 percent, it ultimately began to move back up. But it took more than a year to regain all the ground it had lost. There was plenty of time to analyze the situation, look for an upward trend, and buy into the market while prices were still depressed.

As an investor, my biggest weakness probably has been my impulse to buy a stock shortly after a steep drop. I owned a couple hundred shares of generic drugmaker IVAX when it was trading in the 20s. When the company issued a disappointing earnings report, the stock suddenly plunged to $15 a share. I watched for a couple of days, and saw that it was hovering around $15 or $16, and decided to double up my holdings before it moved back up. It never did. At last check, the stock had dropped another 60 percent to about $7 a share.

Certainly, there are times when a fallen stock can rebound quickly. But, just in case things go the other way, there's one precaution you can take to ensure that you won't get burned too badly. Have your broker put in a *stop-loss order* to sell the stock if the price keeps dropping. For instance, let's say you buy ABC stock at $15 a share after a steep drop. You could put in a stop-loss order at $12, so that if it drops another $3 (20 percent), you automatically sell out at a small loss rather than ride it down 50 or 60 percent (like the IVAX stock). If the company turns around, you always can buy back into the stock later. Just don't rush it. Stocks, after all, fall faster than they rise.

54.

The market always gives you
a second chance.

—Wall Street adage

If you follow a stock closely, you probably have a pretty fair idea of its trading range. If you're looking to buy, you might have a lowball price in mind you would like to pay for the stock.

But stocks don't always cooperate. Sometimes they unexpectedly move up a few dollars before you have a chance to buy in at the price you want. If the price continues to climb, you might be better served to forget that stock and move on to another stock. But there is a good chance that if you wait, your patience will be rewarded. The stock market—and all the stocks within it—go through lulls every year. Nothing goes straight up. There's a good chance the stock you want will drop back into your target price range sometime in the next few weeks or months.

In reviewing the performance of the stocks in *The 100 Best Stocks to Own in America,* I discovered that although they are all great companies with outstanding long-term financial track records, they still have a tendency to hit an occasional lull in the market due to cyclical trends on Wall Street. In fact, about 90 percent of the best 100 stocks have had periods over the past decade during which they were trading below their price of two years earlier. It's times like that—when stocks are down simply because their industry sector is out of favor on Wall Street—that you can get great bargains on some great stocks.

55

The secret of business is to know
something no one else knows.

—Aristotle Onassis

Investment managers go to great extremes to try to learn about stocks that no one follows. "We like to focus on small stocks," says Cowen Opportunity Fund Manager William Church, "because the smaller the company, the less research is done on it and the greater the edge we have on the market."

Paul H. Wick, manager of the Seligman Communications and Information Fund, is a regular at technology trade shows, where he can learn firsthand about some of the newer products coming to market. He also reads about 20 different trade periodicals a month, and checks through the returns of about 1,500 stocks every day. "We like to stay on top of everything," says Wick. "We get to know the companies well. I've probably visited 70 percent of the companies in our portfolio. By knowing a company well, [we can] take advantage of volatility in the market. We can recognize buying opportunities and build a position in the stock when it's at a low moment."

Investment manager Lee Kopp looks for good companies that have not yet caught the attention of the big institutions. "We try to find a company that is unrecognized by Wall Street that is coming out with a new product or is establishing some real momentum so that you can get a double-edged play. The double-edged play is in the growth of the company coupled with an expanding PE, which is simply a matter of Wall Street becoming aware of it."

Do you have areas of expertise where you could have an advantage over the rest of the investing public? Consider your pastimes or your profession. You're probably able to recognize successful trends in your industry before Wall Street does. You're also familiar with the other businesses in your industry, as well as your clients and your suppliers. If you notice that one of the companies you deal with has had a successful product launch, you may want to invest in that stock. Or you might notice that one of your customer companies is suddenly swamped with business, and is working its employees overtime. That could be a buy signal. You can get an edge in the market when you invest in what you know.

56.

Follow your bliss.

—Joseph Campbell

As a kid, I made some money with a paper route. Part of my earnings I would spend on a stamp collection, which I hoped would some day make me rich, and part I spent on baseball cards, which I bought strictly because I loved baseball. Years after I left home, my mother shipped me my stamp collection, and threw away my baseball cards—including hundreds of cards from the 1940s that an older neighbor boy had given me. I wish she had thrown away my stamp collection, which, as it turns out, is worth very little, and kept the baseball cards, which would have been worth tens of thousands of dollars by now.

In the stock market, it often pays to invest in what you like best or know best. For instance, if you notice a great new restaurant, a new store, or a new product that you really like, find out if the company's stock is publicly traded, learn what you can about the company, and if you like what you see, invest some money in that stock.

A few years ago, I took my family to a new restaurant called Old Country Buffet. As we discovered, it was a huge cafeteria-style restaurant with dozens of tables. Every table was full, and the line of customers waiting to eat wound all the way out the door. I went back two weeks later in the middle of a Saturday afternoon, and, much to my surprise, the place was packed even then. I learned that the company was locally owned under the name Buffets, Inc., that it was just beginning to expand nationwide, and that the company's stock was publicly traded. At the time, my wife had a CD that was maturing, and she was looking for a place to invest her money. I suggested Buffets, Inc. But of course, since she rarely ever follows my advice, she passed on the stock. Big mistake. The stock price tripled over the next 18 months.

Sometimes you can get an edge in the market simply by investing in what you know, and what you like. Follow your bliss.

57

The consumer is not a moron.
She's your wife.

—David Ogilvy

Uncovering promising growth stocks can often be made easier by tapping the expertise of your family and friends. From your children, you can learn what toys and apparel may be the rage of the youth market, while your spouse can often keep you up-to-date on the adult end of the consumer market.

"In 1990, my wife and my sister kept talking about the Gap stores," recalls Christopher Boyd, comanager of the American Century Ultra Investors Fund. "The stores were packed, and sales were great. That Christmas it seemed like half of our gifts were from the Gap." Boyd bought some Gap stock for the fund and watched it rise from $11 a share in 1990 to $50 in 1992. "Then my wife went back to the Gap stores, and felt that the selection was poor and the stores were empty. We looked at the numbers and found that same-store sales were starting to slow down, so we sold out at $50." Shortly thereafter, the stock took a quick dive to $30 a share.

Aside from your own observations, and those of your family and friends, where else can you find good up-and-coming companies? Here are several sources:

- *Periodicals. Inc.* magazine is one of several business publications that run annual lists of the fastest growing small companies. Trade journals, boring as they may be, are also a great source of little-publicized information on new products and young companies.
- *The Internet.* There are a variety of sites on the Internet that include information on promising young stocks. America Online has a fairly extensive section on stocks, with some special articles on promising companies.
- *Mutual fund holdings.* In my book, *The Hot 100 Emerging Growth Stocks in America,* all of my picks come from examining the leading stock holdings of the nation's top ranked mutual funds. The more funds that list a stock among its top 20 holdings, the higher the stock ranks in the book. And while not all the stocks pan out—even the best mutual fund managers get it wrong from time to time—it's a good way to uncover some great young companies. You can use a similar system. Pick out several top-performing growth funds, and call to request their most recent annual or semiannual reports. The companies will send them to you at no charge (along with a packet of sales literature). The reports list all of the fund's stock holdings. If some of the same names appear on several lists, those are the stocks that probably warrant further investigation.

It may take a little extra effort to find some good stocks off the beaten path, but the returns can make it well worth the trouble.

58.

Instead of crying over spilt milk,
go milk another cow.

—Anonymous

Many investors find it difficult to invest in small emerging growth stocks because of their risk and volatility. Their concerns are certainly justified, but by playing the law of averages, you should be able to select enough big winners to more than make up for the losers that land in your portfolio.

"Portfolio theory teaches us that adding very risky asset categories can in certain circumstances actually reduce the risk of the portfolio and substantially improve the terms of the risk return tradeoff available to investors," according to Princeton professor and author Burton Malkiel.

Throughout the past century, small stocks, on average, have significantly outperformed the overall market. A study by James P. O'Shaughnessy, author of *What Works on Wall Street,* revealed that since 1951, stocks with market capitalizations of under $25 million have grown, on average, about 20 percent per year. That is significantly higher than the roughly 11 percent per year growth of larger stocks. A $10,000 investment in small stocks in 1951—if continually reinvested in small stocks—would have grown to about $30 million by 1998.

The problem, of course, is that while the averages may favor small stocks, great performance as a group doesn't necessarily translate into great performance of small stocks on an individual basis.

The solution: Play the averages by buying several small stocks. You can expect some of those small stocks to drop—bad picks are part of the game—but the law of averages also suggests that some of your other picks will achieve excellent returns.

Consider this: a bad $10 stock, in a worst-case scenario, can only cost you a maximum of $10. But a good $10 stock could very well grow to $50 or $100 per share and beyond. If just one out of every ten stocks grows ten-fold—which is not unusual—you're assured of coming out ahead in your small stock portfolio—even if the other nine stocks drop to just a $1 a share. But the odds are, based on historic averages, that you will do much, much better than that if you pursue a persistent lifetime investment program.

What would happen if you bought a portfolio of six $10 stocks, and half dropped by 50 percent and the other half rose steadily from $10 to $30—three losers and three winners? Add it up, and you'll find that your $60 investment would be worth $105—a 75 percent gain in a portfolio that included just as many losers as winners.

Individually, small stocks can be risky, but by playing the averages and spreading your assets over several small stocks, you should be able to beat the overall market averages with your small stock portfolio.

59.

Only those who dare to fail greatly
can ever achieve greatly.

—Robert F. Kennedy

If you can deal with the risk, there's an easy way to beat the market averages in an up market. But if stocks are falling, it's you who would take the beating.

Through a policy known as a "margin account," brokerage companies allow investors to purchase securities on credit and to use securities already in the account as leverage to borrow more money.

Most firms allow you to borrow up to 50 percent of your account balance to buy more shares (or to use for other purposes). Margin accounts usually offer very competitive interest rates for the borrowed money—similar to mortgage rates. In early 1998, for instance, when mortgage rates were at about 7 percent, most margin accounts were also in the 7 percent range.

How can using a margin account help you beat the market averages? Let's assume you have $1,000 of your own money to invest in the stock of ABC company. At $10 a share, you could buy 100 shares. By using a margin account, at the 50 percent limit you could buy another $500 worth of stock, for a total of 150 shares.

If share prices rise 20 percent over the next 12 months (from $10 to $12 per share), your 150 shares would grow in value from $1,500 to $1,800. That's a $300 gain. Subtract the 7 percent interest charge on your $500 in borrowed money ($35), and your total net gain would be $265. That's a 26.5 percent gain on a stock that went up only 20 percent. You beat the market by 6.5 percent.

The risk, of course, comes when stocks are down. Take the same scenario, only assume the stock loses 20 percent ($300) over a 12-month period. Your total loss, including the $35 interest charge and the $300 stock loss, would cut the cash value of your stocks by $335—33.5 percent of your initial $1,000 investment. Your cash value drops from $1,000 to $665.

If you assume, however, that over time, the market averages will tend to go up, then a margin account can help you beat the averages over the long term. Obviously, margin accounts are most attractive when interest rates are low. If rates are up in the 10 to 15 percent range, margin accounts become very risky because you would need to have at least a 10 to 15 percent gain in the stock to cover the interest. But in a period of low interest and rising stocks, margin accounts are one of the best ways to beat the market.

60.

Experience enables you to recognize a
mistake when you make it again.

—Franklin P. Jones

No matter how diligent you are in researching and selecting stocks for your portfolio, you're going to make some mistakes. It happens to everyone who invests. But the investors who do best in the long run are those who recognize their errors and unload their mistakes quickly.

"I believe my sell discipline is more important than my buy discipline," says John Wallace, manager of the Oppenheimer Main Street Income and Growth Fund. "When I violate my sell discipline, nine times out of ten I live to regret it. I try to get rid of a problem child in my fund before it becomes a juvenile delinquent. We may buy a stock because of a company's new product or because it has a new management team. But six months later, if the product isn't selling or the new management team leaves—in other words if [the company] is not generating the returns we expected—we will sell the stock."

Todger Anderson, manager of the Westcore Midco Growth Fund, also tries to weed out the losers as quickly as possible. "If it turns out our judgment was incorrect and the company comes out with an unexpectedly low earnings report, we'll get out of the stock." He'll also sell out a portion of his holdings in a stock if the price/earnings ratio gets too high, or if the stock grows so quickly that it ultimately accounts for more than 5 percent of the fund's total assets.

Kaufmann Fund manager Lawrence Auriana also watches a company closely to make sure it stays on track. "If there is some fundamental change in the business or the dynamics of the industry, or if the company is not living up to its plan—if it can't implement its business model—then we'll sell the stock."

Likewise, Fred Kobrick, portfolio manager of the State Street Research Capital Fund, is quick to unload stocks that don't meet his expectations. "We're willing to take lots of little losses, but we won't ride a stock down." Other sell signals for Kobrick include changes in management strategy ("We'd rather they would experiment with someone else's money"); price ("If it hits our target price based on its valuation, it's a sell"); and failure to execute ("If profit margins are coming down, key personnel are leaving, products are coming out late, costs are getting out of control, or earnings are lower than projected, those are all signs that the management is not executing").

Your goal should be to accumulate a portfolio of winners. If you mistakenly add a loser to your account, don't ride it down. Dump it and move on to something more promising.

61

The most absurd and reckless aspirations
have sometimes led to extraordinary success.

—Luc de Clapiers, Marquis de Vauvenargues

It may never happen to you, but reckless aspirations really can lead to extraordinary success. If you keep looking, researching, and throwing some money at promising but speculative stocks, you just might hit a home run. It's no way to run your overall investment program, but taking a flier on a small start-up from time to time can certainly add some excitement to your life.

A friend of mine, Judy Gehrke, had an amazing turn of luck in the early 1990s when she was trying to raise some money to buy a house. She and her family were interested in moving to a bigger home in an upscale Minneapolis suburb, but they didn't have the cash to cover the down payment. "I needed about $35,000," she recalls, "and all I had was $2,500. At that point, that was my entire life savings (aside from her company retirement plan). I heard a hot tip on a new company called Casino Magic that was getting set to launch its initial public stock offering. To be honest, I knew nothing about the company, but I also knew that my $2,500 wasn't going to get me anywhere. I really had nothing to lose. So I told my broker to invest all $2,500 in Casino Magic, which was being offered at $5 a share. I was able to buy 500 shares."

Over the next few months, Casino Magic soared from $5 a share to $10, to $20, to $40, to $60, and ultimately, to $72. Within five months, Judy's $2,500 investment had grown in value to $36,000. "That's when I sold the stock, because I had raised all the money I needed to cover the down payment for the house. Fortunately, the house was still available. They took our bid, we put up the $36,000 down payment and moved in, and we're still living in this beautiful house today." And all because of Judy's "absurd and reckless aspirations"—and a whole lot of luck.

As for Casino Magic, shortly after hitting a high of about $79 a share, the stock split three for one but began to plunge, dropping steadily over the next few years. By early 1998, it was trading at just $1 a share.

No investment adviser would ever recommend betting all your money on a single speculative stock, but every once in a while, it might be fun to take a flier on a few shares of a speculative stock just to see if you can repeat the magic of Casino Magic.

62.

He did nothing in particular and
did it very well.

—W. S. Gilbert, *Iolanthe*

There's no question, stock market investing can be a lot of work. If you've tried it, and you find you don't enjoy it, maybe you would be better served to take the lazy approach to stock market investing. Instead of trying to maintain your own portfolio of winning stocks, a better approach for you might be to invest in mutual funds. Mutual funds enable you to participate in the stock market without the trouble of tracking the market, researching new stocks, and making all the buying and selling decisions.

Mutual funds offer several benefits:

- *Instant diversification.* When you invest in a mutual fund, you become a shareholder of a portfolio of dozens or hundreds of different stocks. That way, you don't have to worry about the volatility of a single stock. Your investment will spread out across a wide universe of stocks.

- *Professional management.* A professional portfolio manager handles all buying and selling of stocks in the fund, as well as all the other day-to-day responsibilities, leaving you to lead your life of leisure.

- *Low fees.* About half of the 8,000 mutual funds on the market are known as "no-load funds" because they charge no fee to buy or sell shares of the fund. Investors are, however, assessed a very small annual management fee of about 1 to 2 percent of assets to cover fund expenses. "Load" funds charge a front-end (or redemption fee) ranging from about 3 percent to 8.5 percent. In most cases, your bias should be toward the no-load or low-load funds. Studies have shown that the no-loads tend to perform just as well as the load funds, so why not save on the up-front fees?

- *Variety.* You can invest in a wide variety of stocks and bonds through mutual funds. There are funds that specialize in small stocks, large stocks, specialty sectors, high yielding stocks, international stocks, and a whole range of bonds and balanced stock and bond portfolios. You can have a strong position in nearly every type of stock, both foreign and domestic, just by buying a handful of mutual funds.

Mutual funds may be the lazy way to invest, but they still provide excellent returns. Build a portfolio of strong mutual funds, and you'll do very well doing nothing at all.

63

The winds and waves are always on the
side of the ablest navigators.

—Edward Gibbon, *Decline and Fall of the Roman Empire*

With more than 8,000 mutual funds on the market, the most difficult aspect of mutual fund investing is deciding which funds are best
for you.

There is a wide range of books and magazines that rate mutual
funds, including my book, *The 100 Best Mutual Funds to Own in America* (Dearborn Financial Publishing). *Money, Forbes, Barron's,* and
Consumer Reports are among the magazines that publish periodic
mutual fund ratings. Most should be available at your library. Regardless of which source you use, there are several key factors you should
consider in deciding which funds are right for you.

- *Five-year track record.* Rarely do the best funds from one year
  lead the market the following year. For investors, it would be a
  big mistake to choose a fund based on its performance over just

12 months. Instead, compare fund performances over a five-year period. You want a fund that has been one of the top performers in its category over a five-year period *and* has done well relative to the market year in and year out.

- *Same fund manager.* A mutual fund is a reflection of the fund manager. Before you select a fund based on five-year performance, be sure the manager who established that record is still managing the fund. If he or she has moved on, so should you.

- *Fees.* All other factors being equal, you should select the fund with the lowest fees. Choose no-load funds over similarly performing load funds. There are plenty of great no-load funds from which to choose.

With a little research, you can accumulate a portfolio of all-star funds managed by some of the ablest navigators in the investment business.

64.

There is nothing that fails like success.

—G.K. Chesterton

The single factor most likely to turn a great mutual fund into a mediocre one, strangely enough, is the fund's own success.

The more successful a fund becomes, the faster its assets grow. In fact, not only does it grow from within through the savvy investments of its manager, it also grows from without through the inevitable flood of new investors attracted to the fund's sterling track record. Once lean and mean, many popular funds quickly become obese and no longer able to maneuver lithely through the market. That's why many funds close their doors to new investors after their assets reach a certain level.

Oversized funds face a couple of significant drawbacks, including a dwindling universe of investment choices, says Princeton professor and author Burton Malkiel.

"Mutual funds usually operate with two constraints," says Malkiel. "First, they will want to limit the holdings of any individual security in their portfolio to at most 2 to 5 percent of their total portfolio to maintain proper diversification. Second, they will usually be unwilling to hold positions representing more than 5 to 10 percent of the firm's outstanding shares to ensure adequate liquidity should the fund wish to sell the shares. Together, these constraints sharply limit the number of companies available for investment."

Malkiel cites a study by John Bogle, chairman of the Vanguard Group, that illustrates the constraints imposed on large funds. A fund with $1 billion in assets and a 2 percent maximum holding in any individual stock could invest in any of about 2,644 stocks if the fund is willing to hold 10 percent of the company's capitalization, and 1,850 stocks if the limit is set at 5 percent.

But for a fund that has grown to $20 billion, the comparable numbers are 352 and 182 companies, respectively. "In other words," says Malkiel, "growing from one to $20 billion in size is likely to reduce the number of securities for purchase by as much as 90 percent."

Size brings yet another drawback as well adds Malkiel. "Moving substantial blocks of securities around tends to move market prices. The funds will be able to take on a large position only at a premium from going market prices, and to liquidate that position only at a discount."

What does that mean for mutual fund investors? You should continue to look for funds with stellar track records, but—with all other factors being equal—you should favor the funds with the smaller, more manageable asset base. There are plenty of good funds with solid track records that have assets under management of well under $1 billion.

Avoiding Troubled Waters

65.

We have met the enemy, and he is us.

—Walt Kelly, *Pogo*

No question the stock market has dished out its share of pain over the years, but many of the problems investors endure are of their own making. They think short term. They panic in bad times and sell out good stocks for a loss rather than hold them for the long term. They make decisions to invest thousands of dollars on a hot tip on a company they've never heard of and have never researched.

To succeed in the market, the first thing you need is common sense and the ability to make prudent, educated investment decisions rather than to buy and sell based on hot tips and emotion. You also need the patience and persistence to hold on to good stocks through down times. And you need to be calculating and confident, drawing on the knowledge that, no matter how bad things look, the market will ultimately move back up. It's your money on the line. The more you put into your buy and sell decisions, the more you'll get out of them.

66.

In investing money, the amount of interest you
want should depend on whether you want to
eat well or sleep well.

—J. Kenfield Morley

The more risk you're willing to assume in the stock market, the
greater your potential for reward. Spend your life investing in small,
emerging growth stocks, and you'll no doubt endure years of volatility.
But in the end, your returns will be astronomically higher than they
would have been with "safe, steady, secure" money market accounts or
certificates of deposit.

Some aggressive investment advisers recommend that stocks con-
stitute as much as 100 percent of an investor's portfolio because of the
superior long-term track record of stocks over other types of investments. Extreme as it sounds, it's a strategy that probably would pay off
very well over a lifetime—except for a little matter known as "peace of
mind." For your own peace of mind, it's nice *not* to have every dollar
you've ever saved riding on a wave as rocky and unpredictable as the

stock market. For your own peace of mind, it's nice to have some money tucked away in other places.

How much risk can you handle? It's a question only you can answer. If you can't sleep nights because you're worried about the ups and downs of one of your aggressive growth funds, or if you get in a foul mood—even around friends and family—every time the market takes a tumble, maybe you should consider rearranging your investment portfolio.

Money—and that ongoing quest for maximum total return—is certainly important. But your health is more important. If you can't sleep at night, or if you're suffering through mood swings and bouts of depression related to your stock investments, you're paying too high a price for whatever financial returns you may be earning. Lighten the risk, even if it means losing a couple of percentage points on your total return. The real return for you will be your long-term health.

What percentage of stocks and stock mutual funds should you hold in your retirement portfolio? Here are some suggested diversification levels for investors at a range of ages:

- *Ages 20 to 39.* Stocks and stock mutual funds, 75 to 100 percent (with money markets, CDs, bonds, and other types of investments comprising the balance), heavy weighting in smaller stocks and stock funds (40 to 80 percent of your stock portfolio, with the balance in bigger blue chip growth stocks)
- *Ages 40 to 55.* Stocks and stock mutual funds, 60 to 95 percent (with about 30 to 75 percent of your stock portfolio in smaller stocks, and the balance in blue chips)
- *Ages 56 to 64.* Stocks and stock mutual funds, 50 to 85 percent (with 25 to 65 percent of the stock portfolio in smaller stocks, and the balance in blue chips)
- *Ages 65 and up.* Stocks and stock mutual funds, 30 to 75 percent (with 10 to 40 percent in small stocks, and the balance in blue chips and utility stocks)

67.

Sometimes the best investments are
the ones you don't make.

—Donald Trump

In the U.S. stock market, an investor with money in hand is like a kid in a candy store. There are well over 10,000 stocks and about 8,000 mutual funds to choose from. To put it lightly, you can afford to be picky. If your broker is pushing you to buy a stock or mutual fund that you're not comfortable with, don't buy it. Insist on looking at other options.

If you're offered a complex packaged investment—perhaps one that combines stocks, options, and derivatives—look it over, but don't commit until you understand exactly how it works and why the broker thinks it's right for you. If your broker can't explain it, don't buy it. Investors have lost millions of dollars on complex investment deals that were high on commissions but low on returns.

Make sure you understand exactly what you're buying. Be choosy. There are a lot of great investment options out there, and you want your portfolio to be stocked with investments that you understand and feel comfortable owning.

68.

Too bad the only people who know how to run the country are busy driving cabs and cutting hair.

—George Burns

Unless your cab driver works the area around Wall Street, he probably shouldn't be your first source of investment advice. In most cases, by the time the hot-tip circuit makes it deep into the general public—to your barber, your butcher, your taxicab driver—the game's over for that stock. As they say on Wall Street, "What everyone knows isn't worth knowing."

There's also a pretty good way to tell that a bull market rally is about to run out of gas. Whenever *Time* or *Newsweek* runs a cover story on stocks, that's a good sign that the market is just about to peak, and the next big correction is just around the corner.

The public popularity rule even applies to mutual funds, according to Princeton professor and author Burton Malkiel. As he points out, the Fidelity Magellan Fund, which is world's biggest fund, has seen its performance decline as its popularity increased. "In the early years of the fund, when its assets were less than a billion dollars, performance was outstanding. The fund beat the market over three-year periods in the late 1970s and early 1980s by 20 to 30 percentage points per year."

But as the fund ballooned with additional investment dollars—it now has assets of over $40 billion—the performance began to decline. "The three-year performance through 1996 was substantially worse than the Standard & Poor's 500 Index and, despite improvements in 1997, the Magellan Fund has remained 300 basis points (3 percent) behind the Vanguard Index Trust 500 portfolio."

Next time you hear a rash of hot tips about a certain stock or a sector, consider it a sign of eminent danger, and make a point of looking elsewhere for your next investments.

69.

Don't ever take a fence down until you
know the reason why it was put up.

—G.K. Chesterton

Sometimes what looks like a bargain in the stock market is really no bargain at all, but big trouble in the making.

Has this ever happened to you? You follow a stock for a period of time, getting a feeling for its normal trading range. Then one day you notice the price beginning to drop. You continue to watch, and the price continues to fall. You check its financials and see that its most recent earnings report was positive. The price continues to drop to the point where you can no longer resist. You call your broker and buy some shares at bargain basement prices. Except that, after you buy it, the stock falls even further. Only when its next earnings report comes out do you realize why the stock had dropped so dramatically. As the new report undoubtedly reveals, the company has hit some serious financial turbulence.

James Crabbe of the Crabbe Huson Special Fund examines a falling stock very closely before deciding whether to invest. "We're not going to invest in that stock unless we've figured out why and how the company is going to bounce back. Maybe it's new management, maybe it's a new subsidiary, maybe it's a new product, or some cost-cutting measures. Only after we've figured that out will we buy the stock."

Be very wary of stocks that unexpectedly begin to fall—particularly during a period when the overall market is moving up. The company's most recent earnings report may be of no value to you in assessing the strength of the stock because the problems are probably more recent. You need to dig deeper. You can call the company and talk with the investment relations manager (don't be shy—his or her job is to deal with investors like you), or search for recent news on the company at the library or on the Internet. Chances are, there's a very good reason for the drop in price—and a good reason for you to stay clear of the stock. But if you find that the company is still doing well, and the price drop is just part of the normal ebb and flow of the market, it could be a good time to buy some shares of the stock at bargain prices.

70.

He has all of the virtues I dislike and
none of the vices I admire.

—Winston Churchill

Sometimes you have to look beyond a company's bottom line to decide whether you want to own its stock. If you don't like the company—no matter how healthy its earnings—don't buy the stock.

It's for that very reason that many investors have declined to own the most profitable stock on the New York Stock Exchange. Philip Morris has led the market in total shareholder return for the past 60 years. But because it also happens to be the world's leading cigarette producer, many investors refuse to own the stock.

Investors have had other socially responsible reasons, as well, for steering away from certain stocks. Teetotalers sometimes avoid the stock of brewers such as Anheuser-Busch. (On the other hand, a lot of Bud drinkers own the stock because they love the beer.) Environmentalists often refuse to buy stocks of companies that are notorious for polluting the environment. Pacifists typically decline to invest in the stocks of weapons manufacturers. Many Southern Baptists refuse to own Walt Disney stock because of the company's flexible policy toward gays.

Of course, you really don't need a reason of conscience to decline buying a specific stock. You might decide against investing in a retailer because you don't like its stores, or a restaurant because you don't like its food. McDonald's stock has been riding high for years, but personally I've never been interested in owning it because, well, let's just say the expression "Big Mac attack" has a whole different meaning to my digestive system. You might not invest in a manufacturer because you don't like its products. I have a friend who refuses to buy Microsoft stock because she owns an Apple computer and has always considered Microsoft the enemy.

Personal preference should be a part of the stock selection process. It's your money. Invest it in the stocks of companies you like.

71.

It is easier to stay out than get out.

—Mark Twain, Pudd'nhead Wilson

One of the best things about the stock market is the liquidity. You can get out of a stock on a moment's notice. A quick phone call to your broker—or a few keystrokes over the Internet—and you're out of the stock. Not all investments are so simple.

Occasionally, your broker or a business associate or even a relative may come to you with a business deal that would require a substantial up-front investment on your part. And unlike stocks, these deals are far from liquid. You're often expected to keep your money in the venture for several years. With private investment deals—unlike the stock market—there's no ready market to sell your shares. If you want out, you have to find someone willing to buy your shares at whatever you can persuade them to pay.

For affluent investors, throwing some money at a few private ventures may make sense. Occasionally there's big money to be made in these deals. But for smaller investors with limited resources, it's much easier to stick with stocks. Only after you've built a strong portfolio of great stocks, such as Microsoft, Coca-Cola, Merck, or Gillette, should you begin to consider investing your money in a private deal.

A friend of mine was persuaded by some business associates to invest a large share of his savings in a start-up company that made an ice cream cookie it planned to sell through Dairy Queen franchises. My friend made the investment after much consideration, and spent the next three years agonizing over whether he would ever see his money again. Ultimately he found a buyer for his shares, and sold out at a profit. His return—about 15 percent annually—was certainly acceptable by investment standards, but for all the risk and aggravation, he would have been better served to stick with stocks.

Even the affluent can find themselves on the short end of some speculative business deals. Professional athletes are notorious for blowing their money on private business ventures that go under. Basketball great Kareem Abdul-Jabbar, the all-time leading scorer in professional basketball history, made millions of dollars throughout his NBA career. But at the age of 40, he found himself buried in debt, thanks to bad deals and poor money management. Fortunately, even at that late stage of his career, Abdul-Jabbar was able to lace up the Nikes to play for a couple more years and earn a few million dollars more to put his financial life back in order.

But unless you're 7 feet, 3 inches tall, with a wicked skyhook, you probably don't have that same option. So be wary of business deals that are easier to get into than out of. Keep it simple.

72.

If you keep your mind sufficiently open,
people will throw a lot of rubbish into it.

—William A. Orton

Would you like to earn an extra $15,000 a week working out of your house in your spare time? Of course you would! And you could, too, through the magic of multilevel marketing—if only the earth's population were expanding exponentially year by year.

Not to paint the entire multilevel marketing industry with the same cynical brush—certainly there are some success stories, as Mary Kay Cosmetics' fleet of pink Cadillacs attests—but if you ever do find yourself buying into one of the more than 500 multilevel marketing organizations in America, do yourself just one favor: Don't quit your day job.

When you "invest" in many of these "business opportunities," what you are actually doing is placing your faith in the "greater fool theory," because to succeed in multilevel marketing, you need to recruit a whole new generation of fools still greater than you. That's where you make your money. Your earnings come as a percentage of the investment money you generate by signing new recruits—and from the money your recruits generate by finding their own recruits. The whole system hinges on constantly bringing in fresh bodies. Generally new recruits are required to ante up an initial investment ranging from several hundred to several thousand dollars. That covers the cost of admission, training tapes, and, generally, some products you have to figure out how to sell.

Where do you find your recruits? Some of the top producers host free "business opportunity seminars" that they advertise in the newspaper. But most people start by pitching their friends and relatives, and, after that fails, they move on to anyone else they know or meet.

I got a call once from a portrait photographer I had used a few years earlier. He said he had a business opportunity he wanted to talk to me about, and wondered if he could stop by the house. He arrived in suit and tie with a briefcase in hand—not the image I remembered of this casual, laid-back photographer.

As we sat down at the dining room table, he began peppering me with questions. How was I doing? How was my work going? Was I happy with the kind of income I was pulling in? The whole presentation seemed stilted and poorly rehearsed. Off the cuff, I said, "What is this, Amway or something?"

He looked up in startled disbelief. "Well, uh, actually it is Amway. But . . . uh . . . but Amway has changed. Let me show you." With that, he popped open the briefcase, and began to make his sales pitch. You may hear the argument from the multilevel marketing industry that their real business is selling products to consumers, but this man was not there to sell me soap. There were no free samples in his briefcase. He was there for one reason—to persuade me to become an Amway recruit like himself. He laid on his strongest pitch, as I sat there in stunned silence. Finally, tiring of the presentation, I broke in, "Okay, where do I sign?"

"Really?" he replied.

"No, not really," I answered, as I showed him the door. "Good luck and good-bye." I never heard from him again.

Despite the rosy financial projections that multilevel recruiters boast in their sales pitches, many investors don't even earn back their initial investment. A 1992 survey conducted by the Direct Selling Association showed that almost half the salespeople who responded to the survey earned less than $500 a year, and 90 percent earned less than $5,000.

It's little wonder when you examine the numbers. Your earnings come primarily from commissions off the up-front investments of those you recruit (and those they recruit, and so forth). In a typical multilevel scenario, you might be required to sign 20 recruits before you begin to see a decent return on your investment. For your recruits to succeed, they must also recruit their own 20 investors. That's 400 investors, all of whom must find 20 more willing recruits. The 400 becomes 8,000, which becomes 160,000, which becomes 3.2 million, which becomes 64 million, which becomes 1.28 billion recruits. Even on this planet, the greater fool theory would be hard-pressed to support those numbers. At some point the system breaks down. Chances are when it does, you'll be the one left holding the soap.

That's a tough way to make a buck. Why make it hard on yourself? Take the easy way, and keep your money in the stocks of great companies. Let them do the work for you.

73

The great mistake made by the public is
paying attention to prices instead of values.

—Charles H. Dow

A lot of novice investors like to buy "cheap" stocks. There's
nothing wrong with that, except that "cheap" to them often refers to the
price of the stock—not the value. They like stocks that cost $5 or $10
a share because they can buy more shares.

But experienced investors have an entirely different concept of
"cheap." In terms of value, a $100 stock may be cheaper than a $3
stock. Value investors look for stocks with inordinately low price-earnings ratios—not stocks that sell for a few dollars.

The price-earnings ratio—known in the business as the PE—is the
most commonly used measure of a stock's value. Many investors
decide which stocks to buy and sell based largely on the PE. (The PEs
are listed every day in the stock tables of most major newspapers.)
Investors often watch the PEs as closely as the stock price itself. It's a
measure every serious investor should understand.

Literally translated, the price-earnings ratio means the stock price divided by the earnings per share. For example:

- A $20 stock with earnings of $1 per share would have a PE of 20 (20 divided by 1).
- A $100 stock with earnings of $10 a share would have a PE of 10 (100 divided by 10).

In value terms, the $100 stock with the 10 PE would be cheaper than the $20 stock with the PE of 20.

PEs are a lot like golf scores—the lower the better. Most established blue chip stocks have PEs in the range of 10 to 30. (Value investors would tend to be more interested in stocks with PEs of 10 or under.) In comparing PEs, you might think of buying a stock in much the same way as you would buying a business. If you can buy a business that earns $1 a year for $10 (10 PE), that would seem to be a much better value than to buy a business with that same $1 of earnings for $30 (30 PE).

So why doesn't everyone buy stocks with the lowest possible PE? Because some companies really are worth more than others. Great companies with fast earnings growth command a premium over slow-growing companies, as well they should.

"We're willing to pay a higher PE ratio for companies that are growing at 30 to 40 percent per year than companies growing at 10 to 15 percent," says Lee Kopp, one of the nation's top-ranked money managers the past ten years.

Kopp says that, to be fairly priced, a stock's PE should roughly reflect its earnings growth rate. "The suggestion from Wall Street is that if the earnings are growing at 30 to 40 percent, you can apply a 30 to 40 PE multiplier. If it's growing at 15 percent per year, you can apply a 15 PE multiplier."

But Kopp concedes that selecting stocks based on PE ratios can be tricky. "When you look at PE ratios, every industry has a different average," explains Kopp. "The biotech industry may sell at an infinite price-earnings ratio because there may not be any earnings. A more mundane industry might sell at an average PE ratio of seven. So you really have to look at the average of that industry."

Perhaps the best point of comparison is the stock's own historical PE ratios. If a stock has had a 20 PE through most of its history, then you would probably be safe to buy the stock at around 20 or less (assuming its earnings are still about the same). If the PE has climbed closer to 30, you might be better served to look for other opportunities and wait for the PE of that stock to drop back down to its normal range.

But one thing you should never do is judge a stock by its price alone. Even if you have only $1,000 to invest, you still need to make your buying decision based on the stock's value, not its price. There is no rule that says you have to buy an even lot of shares. It's totally irrelevant. Odd lots are just as easy to buy and sell as even lots of 100 or 1,000. Look for the best stock at any price. If your choice is between buying ten shares of a $100 stock with a growth rate of 20 percent and a PE of 20, or buying 200 shares of a $5 stock also with a growth rate of 20 percent but with a PE of 30, the choice is obvious. You buy the "cheap" stock—the $100 stock with the lower PE.

74.

He who wants a rose must respect the thorn.
—Persian proverb

If you want to own the stock of a fast-rising company, you'll have to pay a premium. Just be careful not to pay too much. The higher the stock's price-earnings ratio, the more you stand to lose if the earnings suddenly go south.

"A high PE stock that is starting to lose growth momentum can spell trouble," says American Century Ultra Investors Fund Comanager Christopher Boyd.

Some of the highest flying stocks of 1996—when the technology sector was skyrocketing—became some of the biggest losers of 1997 when many of those stocks returned to earth. In many cases, the stocks fared poorly not because of any weakness in their earnings, but because of their exorbitant PE ratios. In fact, in some cases, the stock price dropped even though earnings continued to rise:

- PairGain Technology, for instance, dropped from $30 a share to $19 in 1997 even though the company's earnings grew about 50 percent (through the first three quarters of 1997). But the stock's 75 PE was too rich for Wall Street, which drove it down to about 30 by the end of the year.
- APAC Teleservices, which had a PE of about 80 at the end of 1996, saw its stock price drop from about $38 a share to $13.50 in 1997, even though its earnings remained about the same. Its PE dropped from 79 to 23.

Stagnant earnings can reap similar results. Ascend Communications, which had an 89 PE in 1996, saw its earnings flatten out in 1997 (although its revenues continued to climb), leading to a plunge in share prices from $62 to about $25.

The disaster can be even more dramatic for high PE stocks that suddenly see a drop in earnings:

- Shiva Corp., a computer networking company that had a 65 PE in 1996, saw its earnings drop from 54 cents a share in 1996 to a loss of about 40 cents a share through the first three quarters of 1997. The result was a 75 percent drop in the stock price, from $35 to $8 a share.
- Oxford Health Plans, which had a 55 PE in 1996, reported a 99-cent loss in the third quarter of 1997. The bad news sent the stock tumbling from $59 at the start of 1997 to just $15.50 at the end of the year.

If you want to own some of the market's fastest growing companies, you'll have to accept a fairly high PE. But be sure the PE isn't completely out of whack, because the higher the PE, the greater the chance of a dramatic decline in the stock price if the company's earnings growth suddenly starts to slide.

75.

The object of war is not to die for your country,
but to make the other bastard die for his.

—General George S. Patton

From time to time, the price-earnings ratios of an entire sector become irrationally high. If you own stocks in an overpriced sector, you can save yourself some heavy losses by unloading those stocks before they begin to plummet.

There have been several times in recent history when PEs of certain stocks became dangerously high. Those times are usually easy to recognize because the rationale for the high prices from the experts on Wall Street is almost always the same: "This time it's different. These stocks can support exorbitantly high PEs because . . . [fill in the blank]."

Don't believe a word of it. Their decline is imminent.

Here's a brief history lesson: In the early 1980s, high-tech start-up stocks and biotech stocks were the rage with investors who believed that there could be no end to their spectacular growth. Little matter that many of those companies still had no earnings, or very small earnings, and no track record. Investors were still bidding up the prices. PE ratios climbed into the 50 to 100 range. And the rationalizations from Wall Street's experts began. "These stocks are different from the blue chips. They can support higher PEs because of their potential for rapid growth." When the rapid growth never materialized, investors lost interest in the sector, and prices fell through the floor. Stocks trading at one point as high as $30 or $40 a share were suddenly going begging at $6 or $8.

In the late 1980s, Japanese stocks roared to record levels. Many stocks carried PEs as high as 100 to 200, levels virtually unheard of in the history of the stock market. But unfazed investors continued to buy, while Japanese brokers continued to tout the stocks. "This time it's different," they would say. "This is the great Japanese financial empire, an empire that is taking over the world's financial markets, the world's manufacturing markets, and the world's high-technology markets. These stocks can support the higher PE ratios because they are part of this great Japanese economic machine." And suddenly the machine ground to a halt, the bottom fell out of the Japanese economy, and hundreds of stocks dropped to a fraction of their former highs. A decade later, Japan's Nikkei Stock Exchange is still trading at about half of what its peak levels were in the late 1980s.

In 1991, medical stocks suddenly caught fire. Merck climbed 80 percent. Pfizer went from $40 to $84 a share. Stryker went from $16 to $50. Across the board, medical stocks were climbing far faster than the market averages. PEs were moving into the 40 to 70 range. And again, the rationalizations from Wall Street analysts began to fly. "This time it's different. The world's population is aging, and the need for medical products will continue to expand. That's why these stocks can support high PEs." But in 1992, when presidential candidate Bill Clinton began talking about health care cost containment, Wall Street began to take another look at medical stocks. And suddenly, those stocks began to slide, and continued to slide for about two years to the point where great stocks with great earnings such as Merck and Bristol-Myers were actually carrying PEs in the low teens. They went from overpriced to underpriced, until Wall Street finally rediscovered them in 1995 and pushed their prices back up to fair market value.

If you own stocks of a sector with PEs that seem way out of line, be prepared to lighten your position. Your sell signal will be those wise words from Wall Street, "but this time it's different." When you hear that, get out, take your profits, and move on. Invoke the "greater fools theory" to your own benefit, and let the next guy take the fall. Or as General Patton would put it, "Let the bastards eat lead."

76.

I'm not cheap, I just want a good deal.

—Dennis Kleve

It pays to shop around in the stock market. If stocks with high price-earnings ratios have you worried, you might consider the other extreme—low PE stocks, the stocks that no one else wants.

Some money managers specialize exclusively in low PE stocks with good success. In fact, studies have shown that low PE stocks, as a group, tend to outperform the overall market. "There is some evidence that a portfolio of stocks with relatively low earnings multiples has often produced above average rates of return," says Princeton professor and author Burton Malkiel. "It has also been found that stocks that sell at low multiples of their book values have tended to produce higher subsequent returns, a finding consistent with the views that Graham and Dodd first expounded on in 1934 and were later championed by Warren Buffett. I would point out, however, that stocks that sell at low multiples of earnings and book values may indeed be riskier."

Money manager Lee Kopp points out another drawback to investors who build a portfolio of low PE stocks. "They're missing out on some great opportunities. They have their heads in the sand." If you stick with low PE stocks, you'll never own the great companies. They always command a premium. You'll never see companies like Coca-Cola and Microsoft in your broker's bargain bin.

But for short-term investments, low PE stocks can provide some surprising returns. Don't build your entire portfolio around them, but if you keep an eye out for low PE stocks, you might be able to catch some big gains on the turnaround.

Where can you find low PE stocks? PE ratios are listed in the stock tables of the *Wall Street Journal, Investor's Business Daily,* and most major newspapers. An easier way to find cheap stocks is through the *Value Line Investment Survey* (which should be available at your public library). Value Line publishes a list of the lowest PE stocks in each of its weekly updates.

In 1997, the lowest PE stocks had a banner year. Following is a list of the lowest PE stocks of 1997 and their stock growth through the final nine months of 1997.

Growth of Stocks with Low Price-Earnings Ratios—1997

Stock	PE (3/97)	Stock Price (3/97)	Stock Price (1/98)	%Gain (Loss)
Tucson Electric	4	$14	$18	29%
Chrysler	6	31	35	13
Handy & Haman	6	16	32	100
Perini	6	8	9	12
Webb	7	16	26	63
Unicom	7	22	31	41
Niagara Mohawk	7	9	11	22
Northwest Airlines	7	41	48	17
USX	8	30	30	0
Lamson & Sessions	8	8	5.50	–31
Alaska Air	8	27	39	44
Texas Instruments	8	28	48	71
Bear Stearns	8	30	46	53

77.

You can't lose money taking a profit.

—Wall Street adage

Even with your best stocks, it can sometimes pay to sell out some shares, take the profit, and move some money into other investments. Investment manager Lee Kopp, who was recently rated the top money manager in America, says he sometimes sells out a portion of his holdings in his best stocks for no other reason than to add more balance to the portfolio. When one of his stocks rises quickly, it can suddenly account for a disproportionately high percentage of the portfolio's assets. "At times like those, it can be prudent to pare back your winners. But do it softly," he advises, "because it's hard to find the big winners."

There are also other times when it's good to sell some shares. For instance, if you have a large share of your investment dollars in one stock, and the prospects for that stock suddenly change, you should probably sell a portion of your holdings—even if means paying some hefty taxes on the gains.

A broker friend of mine had a client in the 1970s who owned 4,000 shares of Walt Disney stock, which had climbed steadily to about $120 a share. When the broker heard that business at Disney appeared to be heading for trouble he suggested to his client that he sell some shares and move into something else. The client refused to sell because he didn't want to pay the taxes on the gains. When the stock dropped from $120 to $100 a share, the broker called the client back and asked again if he wanted to sell out part of his position. Again the customer refused, saying "No way. The stock just dropped $20. Let's wait until it goes back up." The stock continued to drop. When it hit $80 a share, the broker made one last appeal to his customer. And again the customer refused to sell because by now the stock had dropped by $40. The stock continued to drop—to $70, to $60, to $50, to $40. Finally, when it dipped into the $30s, the customer called the broker and asked rather desperately, "Well, do you think we should sell the stock now?" To which the broker bellowed, "Not now. The stock's so cheap right now it's a buy—not a sell."

78

Don't you know each cloud contains
pennies from heaven.

—Johnny Burke

William Church makes a living scouring the stock charts for battered market favorites that Wall Street has swept aside and forgotten. The manager of the high-performing Cowen Opportunity Fund concentrates on smaller growth stocks that have fallen out of favor.

"When a stock stumbles, people stop following it," Church explains. "The stock just lays there by the wayside. We like to trawl through those types of stocks and look for companies that may be on the verge of a comeback."

What's the tipoff? Church looks for several traits in a good prospect:

- Companies that are trading near their all-time lows or at least 50 percent below their highs of the past two years
- Companies that are trading at less than two times book value

- Companies that suddenly show some growth after two or three years of flat revenue
- Companies in which the management team is actively buying the stock. ("To us that's a positive. That's real money.")

Church's portfolio is made up largely of companies that faltered either because they had grown too quickly to manage their operations effectively, or because their success attracted competition from larger companies.

"Everybody's looking for the next Microsoft," Church explains, "but it's very rare for a company to go straight to the moon as Microsoft did. Most growth companies hit a point in their development when they begin to stumble." When they do, Church takes notice. Then, just as they appear poised to turn the corner, he loads up at fire-sale prices. Pennies from heaven.

79.

It is better to be a coward for a minute than dead for the rest of your life.

—Irish proverb

Sometimes greed can blur your objectivity. The concept of trying to achieve maximum gain from your stocks is certainly understandable. But there are points in your life when common sense suggests that it's better to lighten your position in a stock than to hold out for an extra point or two and risk losing the gains you've earned.

I have a friend who knows that lesson well. In his late 40s, he had reaped outstanding returns during the big bull market of the 1990s. Although he owned a small portfolio of stocks, most of his assets were in the stock of one company, glass maker Apogee Enterprises. He had built up a large position of several thousand shares of Apogee stock over many years of persistent buying.

Because of his success in the market, my friend decided it was time to retire from his consulting business (at least for a few years) and spend some time traveling and enjoying himself. He planned to sell out a large position of his stocks to raise some cash to pay off his debts and cover his living expenses. He spoke with all of his clients to let them know he would be resigning at the end of the year.

As he planned his early retirement, his Apogee stock continued to edge up, from $18 to $20 to $22 and finally to $23.50. At that point, he decided the time was right to sell. With the gains he had made, he could afford to pay off his mortgage and live well for several years to come. But rather than to sell out at $23.50, my friend got greedy. "I told my broker to sell the stock when it hit $25," he recalled.

The next week, before the stock reached $25, the company issued a devastating earnings statement, reporting massive losses in its construction operation. Over the next two days, the stock dropped from $23 to $9 a share. In 48 hours, he lost more than half of his investment nest egg.

"I still plan to take a couple of years off," sighed my friend, "I can't exactly go back to my clients and tell them I want my job back. But I certainly won't be able to do some of the things I had planned to do. I just have to hope the stock moves back up to $20. I think it will, but it could take a year or two."

No question, he should have sold at $23.50 rather than to hold out for another $1.50 a share. Unfortunately, in the stock market you don't have the luxury of hindsight. That's why, when common sense says sell for the sake of your financial security, don't be a hero. Make the move and enjoy the gains you've earned.

80.

Penny wise, pound foolish.

—Robert Burton, *The Anatomy of Melancholy*

Some investors tend to get caught up in the trading game. They buy a stock, hold it until it has a small run-up, and then sell out at what they consider to be a nice profit. This may seem like a logical strategy—until you look closely at the costs of buying and selling stock.

Consider this example: You buy $5,000 worth of a $50 stock from your broker. The stock goes up 10 percent to $55—pushing your total holdings up to $5,500—a $500 gain.

The only problem is, you have to pay a brokerage commission in the range of $100 to buy the stock and another commission to sell the stock. You also pay taxes on the gain, which could amount to about 35 percent (including state taxes). So by the time you've paid the broker his $200 and Uncle Sam his $100, you have an after-tax profit of $200—just 4 percent.

That's no way to make money in the market. If you have a stock that's doing well for you, stick with it. Hold out for a big gain. A rapid pattern of buying and selling may be a great boon to your broker, but it's a prescription for mediocrity for you.

81.

Don't fall in love with a stock.

—Wall Street adage

For whatever reason, some people get emotionally attached to a stock. If you love a stock because it's made you a lot of money, that's probably a pretty good reason. But some people bond with a stock because they inherited it from a relative and are reluctant to sell it. Sometimes it's because they worked for the company, or have friends or relatives who worked for the company. And sometimes it's simply because they've held the stock for many years and have grown attached to it. Often, people hold onto these stocks even though they may be very poor performers.

If you have a stock in your portfolio that you can't bring yourself to sell for sentimental reasons, here's a little secret for you: The stock doesn't know you own it. It doesn't care about you, it has no emotional attachment to you, and it doesn't have any opinion one way or another about whether you hold it or sell it. So, by all means, sell it. Kiss it good-bye. Get it out of the portfolio and put your money into a stock that has more potential for growth.

82.

Beware the solitary cockroach.
There may be others hiding in the cupboards.

—Gene Walden

The most feared creature on Wall Street these days is the lowly cockroach.

"When a company starts reporting disappointing earnings, we get out quickly," says Seligman Communications and Information Fund Manager Paul H. Wick. "It's the cockroach theory—when you see one, there are probably others coming."

William Berger, founder of the Berger Funds, also prefers to get out of a stock "when the company has earnings surprises that disappoint us. It's the cockroach theory. We think one surprise may beget another surprise, so we get rid of the stock."

Parkstone Small Capitalization Fund Manager Roger Stamper takes the same tack when one of his stocks takes a turn for the worse. "Even if we have to take a 30 percent loss, we'll get out. It's the cockroach theory. I've seen too many times when you wait around a quarter or two to see if the company improves, and it just gets worse."

Even George Vanderheiden, manager of the Fidelity Advisor Growth Opportunities Fund, confesses to a fear of cockroaches. "As soon as I see the first crack, I get out. I want to sell my mistakes quickly. If I buy a stock thinking the company's new concept will do well, and it doesn't work out, I'll sell. Usually the first piece of bad news is not the last piece of bad news."

If many of Wall Street's finest managers, after many years of buying and selling stocks, have all reached the same conclusion, it's probably a strategy you should consider as well. The concept is particularly relevant to smaller growth stocks that can be very volatile.

The cockroach theory makes perfect sense. Most corporate managers try to keep a strong profile for their company. When weaknesses occur, they try to minimize the damage, sometimes reporting only part of the problem in hopes that things will turn around in the ensuing quarters. Most of the time, however, the problems persist and earnings continue to dip, pushing the stock price down even further. So when bad news breaks for one of your small stocks, be prepared to bail out. Otherwise you soon may face an army of cockroaches.

83.

Self-praise is no recommendation.

—Anonymous

Before you invest in a new stock, it's always good to look over the company's annual report. But just remember to focus on substance, not sizzle. Dazzling artwork, flowery praise, and bold predictions are sometimes used to camouflage ho-hum financial returns.

Entire books have been written on how to read annual reports. Many investors like to study every detail of a report's financial section, combing through the balance sheet, the cash flow figures, and the footnotes in search of any undiscovered nuggets that could help them decide whether the company is destined for stellar performance. In truth, that effort probably isn't going to yield anything that the analysts on Wall Street didn't already know months before, but it may be worth your effort for your own peace of mind.

There is probably no one alive who has read more annual reports over the past ten years than yours truly. As the author of *The 100 Best*

Stocks to Own in America (five editions), *The 100 Best Stocks to Own in the World, The 100 Best Mutual Funds to Own in America* (two editions), *The Hot 100 Emerging Growth Stocks in America* (two editions), and several other books on the market, I've read thousands of reports cover to cover. My letter carrier can often be heard muttering profanities under his breath as he lugs the piles of annual reports almost daily to my doorstep. When you read that many reports, eventually you begin to see some patterns that can provide a very quick assessment of the company's financial fortunes.

Typically, you can get a very good indication of a company's success within the first two or three pages of the report, based on what the company chooses to feature up front—or, just as importantly, what it chooses *not* to feature. The deeper you have to page into a report to find anything about the company's financial results, the worse those results are likely to be. But if the returns have been stellar, you can rest assured the company will put it right up front.

If a company is doing well, it will nearly always publish three graphs near the front of the book—one showing *revenue* (or sales) growth over the past few years, one showing *net income* growth, and one showing *earnings per share* growth. When you see those three graphs, invariably they will show steady growth during the years featured.

But if those graphs aren't present, you should be immediately suspicious. It probably means the recent results have been disappointing. Often, companies will put in other graphs in the report instead, such as growth of number of employees, assets, inventory, or cash and cash investments—anything the corporate PR people can come up with to show some type of positive growth. But if the graphs don't cover revenue, net income, and earnings per share, anything else is likely just a cover-up.

Sometimes, the report will open with brilliant graphics designed to convey success. Again, it's just fool's gold, sort of like Hollywood movies—the more dazzling the special effects, the weaker the plot. For instance, in its 1997 report, design software maker Autodesk opened with several pages of colorful, eye-catching, high-tech graphics—but no performance graphs. A look in the back of the report at the company's financial figures showed why. Revenue was down slightly, earnings per share were down 50 percent, and net income was down nearly 60 percent.

Is there anything else worth reading in an annual report? Yes, but rather than to concentrate on the minutiae, investors might be better served to use annual reports to look at the big picture. You probably should spend a few minutes skimming through the balance sheet to see whether the company is showing steady growth in key areas such as assets, sales, earnings, and international operations. You might also take a look at historical price-earnings ratios, book values, and dividend yields to see how they compare to the present figures.

Reports also can give you an idea of what the company does, and of how successful it is at doing it. They often talk about the company's products or services, and they always include a letter to shareholders from the company president, CEO, or chairman that typically gives the most positive possible spin on the company's operations.

If you're really interested in a company's operations, however, you may find the 10K reports to be more helpful than the annual reports. Unlike the annuals, 10K reports have no fluff and no photos—just facts. Printed on plain white paper, with page after page of single-spaced copy, the 10Ks provide a factual profile of the company, with details on its history, its industry, its corporate marketing strategy, its product mix, its distribution system, its customers, its competitors, its employees, its key officers, and its international operations. Any significant lawsuits the company is involved in would also be mentioned in the 10Ks.

How do you get a company's annual and 10K reports? It's as simple as asking for them. Just call or write the company and request their most recent annual report, 10K report, and quarterly reports, and the company will send them to you at no charge. Then it's up to you to read between the lines.

How Far to Trust the Experts

84.

How could I have been so mistaken
as to have trusted the experts?

—John F. Kennedy

It's no secret the experts are often wrong in projecting the future of the stock market. As one investment newsletter writer recently put it, "It's too early to know what lies ahead." Of course it is, but by the time we do know, it will be too late to do anything about it. Opportunity will have passed us by. So the experts do the best they can to provide some direction and insights in this most inexact of disciplines. But mistakes are inevitable. No one gets it right all the time, but some experts seem to have a better handle on it than others.

If you find a broker, a financial columnist, an investment magazine, or an investment talk show you like, stick with it, and learn all you can about the state of the market. You might even be able to get some worthwhile recommendations in the process. But don't expect miracles. These people are human too.

To get the most from the investment experts, you need an open mind and a healthy skepticism. Before you act on anyone's advice, you need to weigh the facts, study the stats, and consider your options. And when you finally do make your decision, it should be based on your own analysis—not the word of a stock market expert. After all, it's your money.

85.

An economist's guess is liable to be
as good as anybody else's.

—Will Rogers

Every month for about four years I wrote a column on global investing for a monthly business magazine. Not to take anything away from the column—because it offered some good information and some pretty good long-term picks for readers—but it did have some flaws that you should know about to understand both the limitations and the value of the business press.

Typically, over the course of a year, I would cover most of the globe (figuratively), writing about stock opportunities in Hong Kong one month, Europe the next. I'd cover Japan, Mexico, South America, the Middle East, Eastern Europe, and any other market that seemed of interest. While not every article was a ringing endorsement of the area's market, I did try to focus on some of the industries or specific stocks of those areas that seemed to have the most potential for growth.

While the information had some merit for the long-term investor, if you were a short-term investor hoping to shift your assets from region to region based on my monthly columns, well, to paraphrase Will Rogers, my guess was liable to be as good as anybody else's.

Here's how the process worked: Near the end of each year, my editor and I decided which countries or regions I was going to cover the following year, and exactly which month each of those columns was going to run. So when subscribers were reading an article about the Brazilian stock market, assuming Brazil to be the hot pick for that month, what they didn't realize was that the article on Brazil might have been scheduled for that issue a full year in advance. In truth, there was nothing timely about Brazil.

All monthly magazines face the same limitations. In its issue directly after the "Black Monday" crash of 1987, *Money* magazine's cover proclaimed "Cash Is King," advising investors to get out of the market and into money market funds. That was strange advice coming at a time when stocks were at rock bottom prices. I later asked one of the *Money* editors about the article. He apologetically explained that the "Cash is King" issue was prepared before the crash, but because of the long lead time needed to lay out, print, and distribute the magazine, it came out after the crash. "That story was intended to warn the readers in advance of a crash," he explained. "We just couldn't get it out fast enough. We would never intentionally have recommended going to cash *after* the crash."

Does that mean you should disregard the personal finance press? Absolutely not. There are several outstanding personal finance magazines. But you need to be aware of their limitations. View them as good advice for long-term investing. Rarely will they contain any "hot" tips that would require your immediate action. After all, the article you're reading may have been assigned a year earlier.

Here are my favorite personal finance magazines: *Money, Kiplinger's Personal Finance, Consumer's Digest, Your Money, Bottom Line Personal, Worth, AAII Journal* (published by the American Association of Individual Investors), *Better Investing* (published by the National Association of Investors Corporation), *Barron's, Personal Investing,* and *Mutual Fund Investing.*

86

Even a stopped clock is right twice a day.
After some years, it can boast of a long
series of successes.

—Marie von Ebner-Eschenbach

Despite the limitations of personal finance magazines, it's debatable whether they are any *less* timely than the myriad investment newsletters that supposedly specialize in timeliness.

For many years, Mark Hulbert has published a monthly newsletter called the *Hulbert Financial Digest* that rates the performance of all the leading investment newsletters. Hulbert's research suggests that, to once again paraphrase Will Rogers, their guess is liable to be as good as anybody else's.

"About 80 percent of newsletters don't beat the market over long periods of time," says Hulbert. "That may sound dismal, but it is no worse than the statistics that apply to any other branch of the advisory industry."

On the bright side, that means that 20 percent of newsletters do beat the market. But as Hulbert is quick to caution, the important factor is whether the 20 percent that beat the market in the past will be the same

20 percent that will beat it in the future. "If there is no such correlation, then it doesn't help us to know that 20 percent will beat the market in the future because it is only randomly related to how they have done in the past," explains Hulbert.

"So the real question is whether there is any correlation between past and future performance. The answer," he concludes, "is yes, although you have to define performance over a long period of time before such correlations exist. If you look at performance over one year or less, there is no correlation. Basically one year is statistical noise. So anyone picking on the basis of one year might as well be flipping a coin. But when you get up to five or ten years, there is a statistical correlation. By betting with the top performers of the last decade and following them through the next decade, you have a chance of beating the odds. There are no guarantees, but you have increased your odds."

Even the leaders, however, can falter. Joe Granville, who was one of the top newsletter publishers of the 1970s, would have cost subscribers who followed his advice through the early 1980s more than 50 percent of their invested assets. And even if the newsletter you buy does beat the odds, there is no assurance that you will be able to duplicate the same performance. For many years, Louis Navellier's *MPT Review* has been one of the top-ranked newsletters in the country, but the typical investor would not be able to follow his recommendations. Navallier's buy and sell lists both feature several hundred stocks each month, and, typically, most of the stocks on the "sell" list just appeared on the "buy" list a month or two earlier. While Navellier has established a strong performance record with his newsletter, it has little practical application for the typical investor who simply can't afford the time, effort, commissions, or principal to trade hundreds of stocks each month.

Regardless of the added costs, heavy portfolio turnover rarely increases performance anyway, says Hulbert. In a recent study tracking many newsletters through several years of performance, Hulbert found that the newsletters that recommended the greatest number of buys and sells tended to do the worst.

"We've also conducted some studies that show that, in the case of most newsletters, if you had bought and held the stocks they recommended at the first of the year, you would have done better than if you had followed all of their trading recommendations buying and selling stocks throughout the year."

No one has a foolproof system. You need to be aware of the limitations of newsletters. See them as a good guide to the market, but not as gospel to be followed religiously.

If you're shopping for a good newsletter, the first one you might consider buying is the *Hulbert Financial Digest,* which will steer you to the newsletters that have rated the highest over the past few years. (For a one-year subscription, send $59 to *Hulbert Financial Digest,* 316 Commerce St., Alexandria, VA 22314.)

Hulbert has several suggestions for investors interested in selecting a newsletter. He recommends you read through several different newsletters to get a feel for the type of advice they offer. Look for several key factors:

- *Risk level.* How risky are its recommendations? "You may find that the letter has done very well over the past several years but its portfolio has been fully margined. You may decide that that's just not for you."
- *Tone.* "If the newsletter does a lot of apologizing, that's a giveaway that they're more interested in protecting their ego than in making you money," says Hulbert.
- *Follow-up.* Does the newsletter tell you not only what to buy but when to sell?
- *Approach.* "In reading the letter, see whether you're comfortable with its philosophy and its writing style or if you find its approach irritating, egotistical, or obnoxious."

Ultimately, you should choose the newsletter that seems to have the most relevance to your own investment situation.

87.

Never trust a man who speaks
well of everybody.

—John Churton Collins

If you can't always get reliable advice from investment newsletters or personal finance columnists, where can you turn?

Some investors like to read through brokerage company research reports to see how professional stock market analysts view a stock. Research reports are sometimes available to investors through their brokerage firm or through the company that is the subject of the report. Many companies will send you free copies of analyst's reports that discuss their stock—or at least they'll send you the reports that paint their stock in the best light. Unfortunately, they are not likely to send the negative reports (if there are any), so you're never quite sure if you're getting the full story.

After years of reading analysts' reports, I've discovered that an analyst's guess (here we go again) is liable to be as good as anybody else's. I've read many a glowing report for a stock that was actually headed for disaster. Just the same, analysts' reports are probably worth reading to give you a better view of the stock and its prospects. But like newsletters and investment columns, analysts' reports are far from gospel.

Some Internet services that track stocks include analysts' evaluations in their stock reports. America Online and Prodigy's Strategic Investor section both include analysts' evaluations in their stock reports. They show how many analysts rate the stock a "strong buy," a "buy," a "hold," a "sell," or a "strong sell."

But even those "buy-hold-sell" ratings are less objective than you might expect, because analysts are discouraged from giving a stock a "sell" rating. Company officers naturally hate sell ratings, and often complain bitterly to a brokerage company that lists their stock as a "sell." They also tend to become less cooperative with the analyst who puts out a negative report, making it more difficult for the analyst to research the company. For that reason, analysts rarely give "sell" ratings. The worst rating most analysts are likely to give most stocks is a "hold." As a result, the entire rating system has been compromised to the point where a "hold" ranking has now become almost the equivalent of a "sell." That's why it's hard to trust any analyst who speaks well of every stock.

88.

If you want something done right,
get someone else to do it.

—Marion Giacomoni

No one ever said you had to go into the world of investing all alone. There is a burgeoning brokerage industry out there dedicated to making investing easier for you. For all the negative press about the brokerage business, the truth is most experienced brokers would do a fairly good job of helping you manage your money. But not all good brokers work well with all investors. Selecting the right investment adviser for you can be a very personal, very subjective process. A broker who may be perfect for one of your friends may be completely wrong for you, depending on your investment objectives, your threshold for risk, and your personality.

If you're going to use a broker, be careful to find one who is ideally suited to your needs. Your broker becomes a vital element of your life, dictating to a great degree the direction and success of your financial well-being and, ultimately, your quality of life (particularly during your retirement years). That's why you need a capable broker who keeps your best interests at heart.

With just a little extra effort you can find the perfect broker for you. Unfortunately, most investors do a poor job of selecting their broker. In fact, most investors have never met their broker face to face, have never visited their office, and wouldn't recognize their broker if they passed him on the street.

Here's how the typical investor selects a broker: He is sitting at home, watching TV, a drink in one hand, bag of potato chips in the other, when the phone rings. From the other end of the line comes the voice of a broker. "Good evening," he says. "I'm John Doe of ABC Investments. If I could come up with an investment opportunity for you with the potential to grow 30 to 40 percent over the next year, would you be interested?"

If the investor says yes, the broker thanks him and hangs up. About two weeks later, the broker calls back and says, "Hello again. This is John Doe of ABC Investments. As you'll recall, a couple of weeks ago when we talked, you said you would be interested in an investment with the potential to grow 30 to 40 percent. Well, you'll be happy to know that I've found a great one for you." The broker explains the investment, and gets the investor's order. Suddenly the investor is hooked, becoming the client of a broker he's never met and knows absolutely nothing about.

That's a very poor way to choose a broker. To do it right, you need to take a proactive approach. Here is a good way to find the perfect broker for you: Start by finding two or three broker prospects by getting referrals from friends, or by attending investment seminars sponsored by brokers. (Brokers often give free seminars to attract clients. Look in the local business press for listings.) When you attend the seminars, if you like the broker and agree with the message, set up an appointment with the broker at his or her office.

When you meet with your broker prospects, ask the following questions. An easy way to remember the questions is to think of "TAPES"— as in "ticker tape":

- *Types of investors.* What types of investors do you work with the most?
- *Approach.* What is your investment approach?
- *Products.* What types of investment products do you specialize in?
- *Experience.* How long have you been a broker? (You probably don't want the most experienced brokers in the firm, because most of them already have hundreds or thousands of clients. But neither do you want a brand-new broker who will make all of his or her mistakes with your money. The ideal broker would probably be one with at least three years of experience. This broker has been around the block, has made some mistakes with other people's money—so he or she has the experience—and yet is still fresh enough in the business to still have some enthusiasm for the job, and for you as a client.)
- *Service.* Rather than ask what type of service the broker will give you, you should set the agenda yourself, outlining the type of service you require. If you want the broker to call you once a week, or once a month, for instance, tell him and get him to agree to your terms in advance.

If the broker answers all the questions to your satisfaction, that's a start. But you should also make sure that you have a good feeling for this person—that you have good rapport, that you trust him or her, and that you feel you could enjoy a pleasant, long-term working relationship with the broker.

You should also take one more step. Call the National Association of Securities Dealers' hotline (800-289-9999). There you can find out if the broker has ever been the subject of disciplinary action, a civil judgment, or a criminal conviction or indictment. Only then, once the broker has passed all the tests, should you sign on as a client.

89.

A burp is not an answer.

—Bart Simpson

A big part of your broker's job is to give you information you can easily comprehend about your account, the trading activity in your account, and the objectives and risks of all of the investment options your broker recommends. You have a right to understand exactly what your money is invested in, and why.

The North American Securities Administrators Association recently issued its "Investor Bill of Rights" to help consumers steer clear of trouble. It states that you have the right to:

- ask for and receive information from a brokerage firm about the work history and background of your specific broker and the brokerage firm itself;

- receive complete information regarding the risks, obligations, and costs of any investment before you are asked to invest your money;
- receive recommendations appropriate for your financial needs and objectives;
- receive account statements that are easily understandable and accurate;
- withdraw your money in a timely manner and receive information about any restrictions on access to your money;
- discuss account problems with the branch manager or compliance department of the firm and receive prompt attention and fair consideration of your concerns;
- receive complete information about commissions, and other sales and service charges, maintenance fees, redemption fees, and penalties; and
- receive enough information from your broker to understand the terms and conditions of the transactions you make.

All good brokerage firms will adhere to these rights. If you believe your brokerage firm has breached those rights, you should transfer your business to another firm that is willing to respect your rights.

90.

I know that you believe you understand what you think I said, but I am not sure you realize that what you heard is not what I meant.

—Berry & Homer, Inc.

If your broker talks in circles, if she talks over your head about investment products she's trying to sell you, if she can't explain, in terms you can understand, how those products work and why those products are right for you, then you need a new broker. The broker's job is to simplify your life, not complicate it. It's a service she is paid handsomely to perform, and one of several benefits you should expect from your broker. If you don't get them, get out.

When you experience any of the following, you should seriously consider firing your broker.

- *Poor communications.* You need a broker who can speak on your level and give you a full and clear understanding of all the investments she recommends for your portfolio.

- *Unsolved operational problems.* If mistakes were made on your statement; if charges were inadvertently added or cash balances inadvertently deleted; if your dividend payments were late in coming; or your verification forms failed to arrive in the mail, you should expect your broker to solve those problems, no questions asked. You don't want a broker who lets problems fester, and fails to keep your account in order.

- *Investments that don't serve your interests.* Some brokers are more interested in their own commissions than they are in your investment returns. Sometimes brokerage firms have special products they push their brokers to sell. Often they are prepackaged portfolios of stocks and bonds that come with a good sales pitch to get them out the door—and a fat commission to encourage the brokers to push them. Or the company may have a large position in a certain stock they want to unload, so managers offer brokers extra incentives to push those stocks. Watch out for those types of investments and the brokers who try to sell them to you. You want a broker who recommends investments that fit your investment objectives—preferably good quality stocks or stock mutual funds that you can buy and hold for the long term. If your broker seems to be more interested in her own returns than she is in yours, it may be time to take your business elsewhere.

- *Lack of rapport.* If you don't feel comfortable dealing with your broker, if she has trouble answering your questions or helping you shape a solid investment portfolio, or if you simply don't like or don't trust your broker, move on. You need a broker with whom you can have a compatible, trusting relationship.

- *Poor performance.* This, of course, is the bottom line. Even if your broker is the nicest person you've ever met, if she isn't making you money, you need to look elsewhere. But be fair. Don't expect every pick to go up—no broker can deliver 100 percent of the time. And don't expect great returns in the middle of a bear market. That's expecting the impossible. What you should expect is that your portfolio stays about even with the market—give or take a few percentage points. When the market is going up, most of your stocks should be going up with it; when the market's going down, you probably should expect to see some of your stocks dropping in price. Riding the ups and downs of the market is part of the game. Over the long term, you should do very well. But if the market keeps going up and your portfolio doesn't go up with it, your broker isn't doing the job. Find someone else who will.

91.

Never mistake motion for action.

—Ernest Hemingway

Just because there's a lot of activity in your account doesn't mean you're making money. All it really means is that your *broker* is making money.

Churning, the practice of trading excessively in a client's account to generate commissions, is the most common violation of the nation's securities regulations. Churning occurs thousands of times a day, and most victims don't even realize it's happening. But if you discover that your broker is churning your account, it may be time not only to fire your broker but to report your experiences to the brokerage company's compliance officer, or even to the Securities and Exchange Commission.

How is it possible that a broker can churn an account without the client realizing it? Here's one way: The broker buys a stock for your account. A couple of weeks later, when the broker realizes that he needs to generate some commission income to meet his company's sales quota, he calls you to present one of three possible scenarios. Depending on how the stock has done, he might say, "That stock we bought a couple of weeks ago has gone up, so why don't we sell out, take our profit, and move into another stock that looks more promising right now." Or, instead he might say, "That stock we bought two weeks ago has gone down, so let's get out of it, and reinvest in another stock that looks more promising right now." Or, finally, he might say, "That stock we bought a couple of weeks ago hasn't moved. Let's sell it out and buy something else that looks more promising right now." So whatever the circumstances—whether the stock has gone up, stayed the same, or gone down, the broker can rationalize a reason for you to sell out one stock and buy another—generating two commissions. You don't want a broker who is constantly urging you to turn over your portfolio. If it happens to you, tell your broker you want him to recommend good quality companies that you can hold for the long term. If he continues to try to churn your account, report his practices to his company, and possibly to the SEC. Then move on to a different broker.

Here are four other common broker violations that you should be aware of. If at any time, you sense that you are falling victim to any of these practices, you should contact the broker's company, and, depending on the violation, the SEC to resolve the problem before it costs you a big chunk of your life savings.

1. *Misrepresentation.* A broker cannot make false or misleading promises about an investment he or she is trying to sell you. For instance, if your broker claims that a stock or stock mutual fund is guaranteed to attain a specific rate of return, that is misrepresentation. Brokers can guarantee the return of some government bonds and insured certificates of deposit, but they cannot guarantee the performance of a stock or mutual fund.

2. *Unsuitability.* A broker who tries to put you into risky investments that are unsuitable for you is violating securities regulations. For instance, if you are retired or nearing retirement, and

your broker tries to sell you volatile penny stocks, options, futures, commodities, or other highly speculative investments, he or she is not looking out for your best interests. The broker is attempting to take unnecessary risks with your retirement dollars, which could lead to your financial ruin. Unsuitability is against the law and violates the rules of the SEC. But unscrupulous brokers continue to push unsuitable investments on unwitting customers because of the high commissions they can earn selling those types of investments.

3. *Unauthorized trades.* Unless you sign an agreement giving your broker discretionary control over your portfolio, the broker is not allowed to make any buys or sells in your account without your consent. If your broker is buying and selling investments for you without consulting with you first, the broker is violating SEC regulations.

4. *Misappropriation.* If it happens to you, God help you. In a few scattered cases, investment managers have fled the country with their clients' money, or have lost it all through bad investments—sometimes hiding the bad news from clients until all the money is gone. If the broker works for a major brokerage firm, it is very likely you would be able to recover most or all of your lost assets—but not without some sleepless nights and a lot of hassle. But if your broker works alone or for a small firm, your money could be gone forever. It has happened before, and it will happen again. That's why the broker selection process is so important. You need a good broker from a well-established, reputable brokerage firm. If you have concerns about the integrity of your broker or his or her firm, take your money while you can and move it elsewhere.

92.

Trust everybody, but cut the cards.

—Finley Peter Dunne

One way to ensure that you don't lose most of your assets to an unscrupulous broker is to spread your assets around. Many investors have more than one broker, or they have some of their investment money with a full-service broker and some in mutual funds or a discount brokerage account they manage themselves.

One good way to use more than one broker is to find brokers who specialize in different areas. For instance, you might have one broker who specializes in large national stocks and another who focuses on smaller regional companies. You'll learn about all of their favorite picks, and you can decide for yourself which ones seem best for you.

Chances are you could do just fine even if you put everything in one account. But you might sleep a little better if you spread your money around—and you might even enjoy slightly better returns.

93

There are worse things in life than death.
Have you ever spent an evening with
an insurance agent?

—Woody Allen

I've got to admit, as much as I've studied the insurance market, I'm still not particularly satisfied with all the choices I've made as an insurance consumer. But here is the advice I continue to hear, and the advice I continue to believe: Buy term insurance and invest the rest yourself.

I've had my share of insurance agents through the house over the years, spending hours flipping through charts and giving their deathly dull presentations. And in every presentation, they show, theoretically, how much I could make and how fast I'd make it if I were to sign up for a certain type of insurance policy they happened to be selling that year. But, in truth, their projections have never come true, and the investment returns on their policies have always been absolutely dismal. What's worse, my agents have always readily admitted their mistakes themselves, using the ploy to urge me to drop the old policy and move to another one that would earn them yet another whopping front-end commission.

Never again.

Here's how you beat the market in the insurance game. You don't. Period. Buy term insurance at the lowest price you can find from a reputable company, and stick with it for life. Don't add universal life or monthly annuities or anything else with a big front-end commission (which would tend to be exactly what your agent will be pushing you to buy). Keep it simple, keep it cheap, keep it term, and invest the rest of your money yourself in stocks, mutual funds, and other traditional investments. By the time you retire, you'll be tens of thousands of dollars ahead.

Maintaining a Healthy Perspective

94.

If you can keep your head when all about
you are losing theirs . . . yours is the
earth and everything in it . . . .

—Rudyard Kipling

Success in the stock market requires a combination of many traits—intelligence, patience, persistence, and even a little bit of luck. But nothing is more important to successful investing than the ability to maintain your emotions through good times and bad.

If you can keep your head when those around you are losing theirs, if you can buy when stocks are down and investors are fleeing the market, and sell when market euphoria has pushed prices up beyond reason, if you can convince yourself to sell your losers and keep your winners, you will enjoy tremendous, sustained success in the market.

Fear, greed, and the other extremes of emotion only get in the way of a successful investment program. If you can keep your cool and make your investment decisions based on solid research and long-term market trends rather than on whim and emotion, you'll be way ahead of the game—and the vast majority of the investors who play it.

95.

The harder you work, the luckier you get.

—Gary Player

There's no guarantee that hard work and diligent research will result in winning stock selections, but like any other pursuit, the more you put into it the more you're likely to get out of it.

Seligman Communications and Information Fund manager Paul H. Wick spends long hours researching the market and the stocks within the communications sector. He attends trade shows and conventions to try to spot the latest technological trends and the emerging growth companies that may benefit the most from those trends. "I also read a tremendous amount, particularly in the trade press—at least 20 different periodicals a month." He also glances through the stock returns of about 1,500 high-tech stocks every day. "We try to stay on top of everything."

Wick travels the country constantly, visiting companies and talking with corporate managers. "We get to know the companies well. I've probably visited about 70 percent of the companies in our portfolio. By knowing a company well, we can take advantage of volatility in the market. We can recognize buying opportunities, and build a position in the stock when it's at a low moment."

"We're out on the road constantly, meeting management, talking to customers, talking to competitors, talking to suppliers," says John W. Rogers, Jr., of the Ariel Funds. "We want to know everything there is to know about that business."

Kaufmann Fund manager Lawrence Auriana and his comanager Hans Utsch meet every day with the management of two to six small companies, talking over the company's business strategy and trying to determine whether the concept will fly in the marketplace. "We already know a lot about these businesses—usually we know more than they expect us to know. In most cases, we've already met with their competitors and their suppliers, and we've followed their industries for years. We can usually tell if their estimates are overly optimistic."

You may not be able to put as much time and effort into your portfolio as fund managers put into theirs, but then you don't need to maintain a portfolio of 100 to 200 stocks, as they do. But before you make a decision to buy any stock, it's probably worth your effort to learn as much as possible about a company to decide whether it is likely to perform well over the long term.

96.

Above all, trust your gut.

—Phil Jackson, *Sacred Hoops*

Long hours of research, checking charts, and reading reports can only get you so far. At some point, the final decision must come from within.

"We call it informed intuition," says investment manager Lee Kopp. "For me, it goes back to 38 years of information, instinct, gut feel, and a host of information coming in."

If the financials check out, if the business concept checks out, if the products or services have a niche in the market, if the management seems competent, then the final decision ultimately comes down to how you feel personally about the company and its concept. If you're not sure, move on. There are thousands of stocks to choose from. But if it's a company you get excited about because of its products or its potential for growth, by all means trust your gut and buy some shares. If you're wrong—and there will be those times—you'll know it soon enough, and you can always bail out. But more often than not, your informed intuition will lead you to some winners.

97.

If I had known I was going to live this long,
I would have taken better care of myself.

—Eubie Blake (1883–1983)

One of the golden rules of investing is to pay yourself first. In other words, before you blow your paycheck on restaurants and entertainment, clothing and vacations, big ticket electronics and home improvements, put some money away.

Less than 10 percent of retirement age people in the United States are financially independent, according to recent surveys. The others live in poverty or survive with help from their families, charities, or government assistance.

Part of the problem is that we don't start planning and saving for retirement soon enough. On average, the typical worker does not even begin the retirement planning process until about three *months* before he or she is scheduled to retire. You need to make retirement savings a priority. Sure, there may be dozens of other things you feel you need—a better car, better clothes, home improvements, the latest electronics, new furniture, etc.—but investment savings needs to be high up on the list.

You don't want to live your retirement years in poverty. Make sure you have a solid and systematic investment program. If you can't do it on your own, set up a mutual fund account that automatically deducts a couple hundred dollars a month or more from your checking account to invest in mutual fund shares.

As tempting as it may be to spend lavishly in your youth, you don't want to be caught short in your old age. The only one you'd be cheating is yourself. Expect to live to a ripe old age, and save and invest accordingly.

98.

Perseverance: A lowly virtue whereby
mediocrity achieves glorious success.

—Ambrose Bierce, *The Devil's Dictionary*

Successful investing need not take a lot of effort nor a lot of expertise. It just takes commitment and perseverance. Anyone can succeed in the stock market. This is not rocket science. You don't have to follow the market every day. You don't have to take big risks. You just have to maintain an ongoing investment program for life. Success for most investors must come over a long period of years. The more you put into it, the more you'll get out of it.

"Everyone's goal," says Franklin Resource Fund Manager Michael Price, "should be patience and risk avoidance, and then let time make you money."

"Our theme," adds John W. Rogers, Jr., of the Ariel Funds, "is slow and steady wins the race. Our logo is a turtle. Our newsletter is called *The Patient Investor.* Patience is very important in successful stock market investing."

There will be some down times in the market. There will be periods, in fact, when you wonder why you're investing in stocks at all. But keep the faith, focus on the long term, and in the end, you will have achieved hard-fought but glorious success.

99.

If all the economists in the world were laid end
to end, they would not reach a conclusion.

—George Bernard Shaw

There has probably never been a consensus among Wall Street economists regarding the future direction of the economy or the markets. One says sell, the other says buy. One says go with stocks, the other says bonds. One says high tech's the ticket, the other says blue chips. The more you listen to the experts, the more confused you're likely to become.

Ultimately, you need only to trust yourself. Become confident in your own decisions based on your own experience and knowledge of the market. Don't chase the hot trends. Don't panic every time a market expert predicts a fall in prices. Develop your own strategies and your own system for playing the market. Because, in the end, there is one fact with which all the experts must agree: Over time, the market always moves up.

100.

It's what you learn after you know
it all that counts.

—John Wooden

You've just read a hundred ways to beat the market. Now you know it all—which, of course, means you're finally ready for the real learning to begin. You can't truly discover how you'll react emotionally to the first big market correction, nor can you measure your own depth of courage to hold on and stick it out through good times and bad simply by reading a book. You can't learn about greed and fear. All you can do is throw yourself at the mercy of the market to find out how you'll react to its many twists and turns. Book knowledge is only the beginning.

"Once you think you've found the key to the market, someone always comes along and changes the lock," says Fidelity's George Vanderheiden. "Successful investing requires imagination, independent thinking, patience, and a touch of contrariness, rather than a mechanistic following of the rules."

Investing in the stock market can be fun, profitable, exhilarating, exasperating, and, at times, downright scary. Try to take it all in stride. See each new twist as another lesson. As Marina Horner once put it, "What is important is to keep learning, to enjoy challenge, and to tolerate ambiguity. In the end there are no certain answers."

Index